Managing
TrumPolitical Projects

Yasser Osman & Yara Osman

ISBN: 978-1-970024-66-1

Table of Content

Preface

Yasser Osman and his daughter Yara wrote their first book, *Buildings, Project, and Babies*, as a professional guidebook for project managers— and a very special kind of project managers at that. They are not the leaders of temporary, task-oriented teams within large corporations, government agencies, or nonprofit organizations that come to mind for many of us. They are not facilitators hired from an outside consulting firm to lead such a team, or even internal executives chosen to lead an important if time-limited "project" on their way up the corporate ladder.

No. They are in fact professionals who create and lead teams that manage the construction of commercial and government buildings, transportation links, or other components that will become, when completed, a new and functioning urban neighborhood, or a retail and entertainment destination for tourists, or an airport, or even a summer palace for a nation's royal family. They come from backgrounds in architecture and design, engineering, business management, or even careers in government administration. They may have an MBA, or an M.Arch., or an MPA, or any number of bachelor's degrees—or no postsecondary education at all. Regardless of their professional experience or educational background, the project managers for whom Yasser and Yara Osman have written their books, including this one, are trusted with enormous responsibility and work all over the world. They learn and grow in their profession through a combination of people skills, technical expertise, and an unfailing commitment to learn from every project they manage, so that their performance on the next one is that much better.

The best of these project managers work on projects of enormous scale as defined in geographic size, total budget, and the impact a completed project will have on the economic, civic, and political life of the country where the project is located. They are an international community of professionals who may complete a project in Indonesia one year and find themselves in Brazil or the Middle East or the United States for their next assignment. Their success or failure has enormous consequences, and yet, until the past few years when political leaders in Europe and the United States came from careers in big business, the public at large has thought little about a profession we might call *international construction and development project management*, or the professionals who work within it.

Yasser and Yara Osman have made it their mission to change that. *Buildings, Projects, and Babies* is more than a guidebook for international construction and development project managers: it is a call for more public understanding of the importance of this profession, and a corresponding investment of educational resources in producing professionals who are more fully prepared for the challenges they will face as international construction and development projects become a more important part of the world economy. Their introductory concept—the startling, compelling, and even humorous analogy they draw between the teamwork involved in creating huge projects and the interactions among the mother, father, doctor, and nurse working together in a delivery room during the birth of a baby—is only the first of several ideas project managers and the public can take from their first book to improve the way international megaprojects are created, the way the teams that manage them are assembled, and the way project managers can work to ensure a successful completion. The difference between "fixed wealth" (the physical assets of construction materials, HVAC systems, completed buildings, road and rail connections, etc.) and "moving wealth" (the human creativity, intelligence, and expertise that is applied to bring a project to successful completion) is one of these important concepts. So is the authors' insistence that there are no such things as "problems" in a construction or development project, since this is a word associated with a high probability of failure. There are only "issues" that can be solved, through teamwork combining elements of moving wealth such as keen observation, learning, creativity, technical skill, and collaboration. There are other big ideas referenced and briefly explained in this book. But for those who haven't read *Buildings, Projects, and Babies*, I highly recommend it.

TrumPolitical Projects is also written to account for geopolitical intrigue. Continuing their call for the commitment of more resources to educate and train professionals in the field of international construction and development projects, Yasser and Yara Osman take the next step of introducing ways these projects have been and can be used to mask larger corrupt or political projects by diverting funds from an "official" project budget to support a separate and secret agenda. It's a serious risk in large international projects, where the budget is large enough for small percentage variances to mount into millions of dollars or more. In countries where governments do not rely on the consent of their citizens but instead are controlled by an elite few, there can be few or even no limits whatsoever on the risk for a project that looks like a luxury shopping mall to be in fact a "front" for the funding of a secret military base in a neighboring country. Or it can simply be a way to siphon off enough cash to build a summer residence for a corrupt government official, or to invest public money in the stock market for private gain.

The authors have based their analysis of these abusive practices on real experience. However, in order to keep the educational message paramount, they have cast their examples in fictional locations instead of telling the literal truth as they experienced it. This fictionalization also reminds us that the practices revealed in this book are not new to our world today, even if the risk of them becoming normalized is more serious than ever. Corruption and secret political agendas are almost certainly as old as the earliest civilizations that have built temples, aqueducts, and city walls. In this book, their examples include a fictional new civic center in a modern South American city, the imagined construction of a port facility at the Atlantic terminus of the Panama Canal during its construction, and in the as-yet unrealized border wall between the United States and Mexico.

The premise of *TrumPolitical Projects* is that project managers are in a unique position to identify, and to then try to make the best of managing, a corrupt or political project. And then some: Yasser and Yara Osman point out the unfair burden this experience puts on an individual project manager, since the forces behind a corrupt or political project are almost always too large for a single individual to fight. This is certainly true in countries without representative governments and the legal and regulatory institutions that would be needed to take on the secret stakeholders behind the secret and distinct projects funded through a project budget that is officially under the control of one of our project managers, but is in fact beyond that manager's control.

This book is not all doom and gloom, of course. It provides new tools for project managers to use in diagnosing whether their projects might have a secret political or corrupt component, and outlines the choices a project manager can make when this appears to be likely. Equally important, it includes an additional way to confront a corrupt or wrong-headed political agenda through an academic analysis of how architects and city planners have addressed design challenges similar to those we face today in different historical times—with varying degrees of success.

Finally, *TrumPolitical Projects* points out that, at least for now, the United States is still a nation where national institutions are strong enough to be brought to bear to combat corrupt or political projects. It may be too late to do this in many real-life projects underway today, or that will be initiated very soon in other countries in the world. If it is remarkable that in a world where doctors, lawyers, and architects all have degrees and organizations that oversee and certify professionals in their field and there is still no formal degree for international construction or development projects, the authors believe that the establishment of this sort of professional education and the creation of a professional governing body is still possible in the United States. And while many countries provide no recourse for project managers who find themselves in the midst of a secret corrupt or political project, the United States is still a nation where a government agency can be established to support these professionals through the investigation of a large construction or development project, with the power to sanction those behind these secret agendas and refocus a project toward its officially stated goals.

The authors have no illusions that there are very real risks that, if nothing is done, project managers in the United States, or project managers from the United States hired to work overseas, will one day be as vulnerable to the whims of secret stakeholders with secret scopes of work as the fictional characters introduced later in this book. But they are optimistic that, with a broader understanding of the true nature of these projects by the professionals in the field and the public at large, something can in fact be done. It's an ambitious proposal written by ambitious authors working in an ambitious field.

Tom Martorelli
Writer and Historian
Winthrop, Massachusetts
June 20, 2017

A Note from the Authors

What do you do when the project you are managing suddenly becomes unrecognizable? Perhaps it is your first day on the job and all is not as it was described by your client when you were being oriented to the project. For example, new team members suddenly appear without your involvement in hiring them, or team members act in ways that make you believe they already know each other, even though no prior relationships have ever been discussed. Or, several months into the project, despite your careful efforts to keep communication channels strong and open among your team members, you are surprised by a sudden and significant change in the project's scope, or schedule, or budget. As the project manager, you are responsible for keeping the project's fixed wealth—its "things" such as the buildings, HVAC systems, and transportation and utilities connections to the outside world—under control. And you are also responsible for managing your moving wealth—the skills, expertise, and ideas of your project team members—in a way we believe is even more important to the ultimate success of your project.

As a good project manager, you have applied your own experience in creating an environment in which both the project's fixed wealth and its moving wealth are delivered, assembled, connected, applied, and directed in a way that gives you and your team the maximum chance of achieving all, or nearly all, of your project's key objectives. Your past experience has proven your ability to do this; it is why you have the reputation for professionalism and even talent as a project manager. Your clients past and present respect you for this, as do members of your current project team and those with whom you have worked in the past. But this time, things are different. Something has gone terribly wrong, and you didn't see it coming. What can explain this shocking development? Have you failed to monitor the project in some fundamental way? Have you neglected team members who needed support and might have helped avert this crisis? What will the impact be on your project, or even the careers of your team members and yourself?

As a seasoned project manager for international megaprojects in the United States, Bahrain, and Qatar, Yasser Osman has found himself in this precise situation, with the same bewildering disconnect between his years of success in the field and the sudden realization that he might be staring failure in the face—with no reason around to explain the situation. In fact, he has experienced it all more than once. How he managed his way through these crises, what he learned from each of them, and how he believes his experiences can be useful for his colleagues in project management is the reason behind this book.

Based on these real-life examples of projects in which secret agendas—the political or corrupt transfer of financial assets through a "normal" international construction project to fund covert military operations; to provide support for government programs without official or constitutional approval; to build a vacation home for a corrupt government official; or even to invest public money for private gain in a business venture or the stock market—coexisted alongside a project's official and public purpose, the authors of this book believe we can help project managers understand the risks they face when a project is not what it seems. And, more importantly, we can recommend a range of solutions for these issues.

Like *Buildings, Projects, and Babies*, the author's first book, *TrumPolitical Projects* is written for project managers. It builds on that first book's central thesis that the events and characters involved in a large international construction or development project can be described using the analogy of a hospital delivery room during the few hours (one hopes) when a baby is delivered.

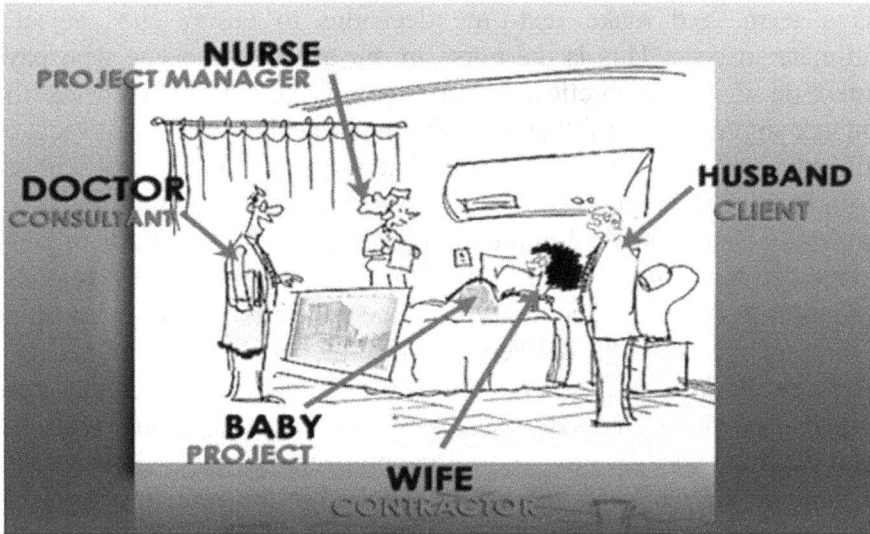

For those who have yet to read it, our premise is essentially that there are four roles in that situation that are similar to members of a construction project team. There is the designer whose original idea, as expressed in architectural plans and specifications, brings a theoretical framework to the project. In our delivery room analogy, this is the doctor, who brings a level of professional and even scientific knowledge to the challenge of delivering a healthy baby.

There is the client or owner, who provides the resources necessary to construct the project's buildings, and who will manage them for their intended purpose when they are completed. This is the father in our delivery room, who is intensely interested in the successful delivery of a healthy baby and is also concerned about minimizing the risks that might get in the way.

There is the contractor, the team of companies with their skilled and unskilled laborers, who actually do the work required to construct the project's structures and in many ways bear the most risk throughout the process. In our analogy, this is the mother, who also does the most work and bears the greatest risk in the delivery room.

And finally there is the project manager, the team of professionals who monitor the activities of everyone on the site, keep them together as a team, and make real-time decisions to ensure the project's ultimate success. This is the nurse in our analogy, the one who pays attention to the theoretical knowledge of the doctor, respects the intense interest of the father in delivering a healthy baby, and most of all, supports the mother in ways that may be routine and without complications, or might also involve complications that must be understood and managed in the minutes or hours the mother is in labor in the delivery room. The nurse is the one individual who needs to pay attention to everyone and everything; he or she is the one who keeps everyone's focus on the delivery of a healthy baby.

Like *Buildings, Projects, and Babies*, this book includes case studies based on the authors' rea-life experiences, along with the introduction of several more generalized project management techniques and concepts that can be applied in the context of projects readers may manage in the future. These include the concepts of fixed and moving wealth; the balance and prioritization of a project's key success factors of money, time, and quality (hint: the most important one is time); the importance of creating an environment for learning in the management of any project team; and the authors' core philosophy that there are no such things as "problems" in the operational life of a project, only "issues." This linguistic distinction is important because in the authors' experience, the word "problem" is often used by team members to describe events or circumstances that cannot be solved and therefore threaten the success of a project; or a "problem" might also be introduced to the team to shift responsibility for solving it away from the team member introducing it, leaving it up to other team members to come up with a solution. An "issue," on the other hand, is always associated with a solution, and—equally important—the authors train their team members to always accompany the introduction of an "issue" in a project with a proposed solution that the team can then discuss and develop before implementing it.

All of these concepts apply to the projects introduced in this second book's fictionalized case studies, as do additional techniques project managers can use to monitor the progress of their work in ways that may help identify the intrusion of a political or corrupt agenda, or to limit the damage this secret agenda can inflict on the project's official or stated bricks-and-mortar objectives despite the existence of a parallel and secret agenda.

Given the delivery room analogy, project managers who find themselves in a project that has a secret political or corrupt agenda are in a difficult situation. We are the nurses in a delivery room, and as noted in *Buildings, Projects, and Babies*, the fact that we are the nurses gives us the ultimate responsibility for managing other members of the team both during the times when all is proceeding according to plan and when at those other, more stressful times when issues arise.

In the case of corrupt or political projects, as we will see in the coming chapters, we find ourselves as nurses in a delivery room where the mother is delivering twins. The additional strain on the mother and the resulting stress on the father and doctor would be enough to manage if the only challenge were the delivery of two babies at the same time instead of one. The truly difficult element of a corrupt or political project is that, after the nurse delivers the first baby—the official scope of work which the project manager can control—the second twin must still be delivered. But when this second baby is born—in other words, when the corrupt or political scope of work is completed—the nurse cannot be in the delivery room, and it may also be true that none of the other team members might be present either. There may be a different father, and there will likely be a different doctor. Without getting too graphic in our delivery room analogy, this second baby will essentially be an amount of money that is taken from the project, to be used to build and operate the second secret project or twin.

As project managers in these situations, all we can do is manage the healthy delivery of the twin we can see. We must leave the healthy delivery of the second secret twin to the secret stakeholder(s) who are responsible for it. We must be careful not to get carried away with wondering about the twin we cannot see—we don't need to take care of that one.

Finally, why, might you ask, is our book entitled *TrumPolitical Projects*? The answer is a bit complicated, but begins with the fact that while this book can be used by project managers anywhere in the world, there are certain aspects of it that are aimed more directly at professional project managers in the United States. The reasons for this focus on the United States are both optimistic, and to a degree, pessimistic as well.

The optimistic reason for our decision to write this book for American project managers is the fact that while we can honestly admit that in certain parts of the world corrupt and political projects are a fact of life that are not only tolerated but supported by the governments of a number of countries—in these cases, project managers have little or no recourse to anyone, government or otherwise, to ask for help if they are facing risk or even danger when their projects are commandeered by secret stakeholders with their secret scopes of work—happily, this is not the case in the United States—not yet. As we will discuss in Chapter 6, there is still time for this country to create standards for professionalism in the field of project management; perhaps establish formal licensing procedures and, even more ambitious, create a federal agency responsible for investigating corrupt or political projects with an eye toward eliminating political or corrupt agendas to support project managers who clearly cannot solve these issues on their own.

The more pessimistic reason for aiming this book at American project managers is that in today's world, two trends that are increasing the risk of encountering these situations in other countries—in which there is little or no governmental protection for project managers who find themselves in corrupt or political projects—will one day be the case for American project managers as well. The first is the simple fact of globalization: as large international projects become more prevalent in an increasingly global economy, it is likely that American professionals will be asked to become members of project teams in other countries and to one day even lead them. We need to be prepared for the risks that await us as we bring our skills and expertise to regions of the world in which the rule of law is different from what we expect here at home. The second is the fact that there is evidence that the government of the United States itself may be embarking on international construction projects whose agenda is more political than economic or civic: and yes, we are talking about the proposed border wall to separate the United States from Mexico. Chapter 5 of this book includes an extensive discussion of how the border wall is an example of how the intrusion of a political agenda in construction and development projects might begin in the United States, and our reflections on the risks and dangers associated with such projects.

Chapter 1
Where's My Penthouse?

"Where in the world have you seen construction people who do everything on time, with good quality and at minimal prices? Just give me one country like that. A country like that doesn't exist in the world, you know. There's not one such country anywhere in the world."
~ Vladimir Putin

"Mr. Gonzalez, you forgot to invite the press." Alessandra Cruz, Roberto Gonzalez's administrative assistant, hurried into his office the day before Gregorio Sanchez, CEO of Latin American Mining and Metals (LAMM), was scheduled to make his site visit to the LAMM Tower in Santa Cruz de la Sierra in Bolivia. The tower would be a gleaming sixty-story structure, the tallest in Bolivia's largest city, which was also Latin America's fastest-growing urban center. While the LAMM Tower stood on what was now the outskirts of the historic center of town, it was the centerpiece of a massive new complex of office buildings, hotels, retail malls, a concert hall, and municipal museum called "El Centro Nuevo," the new downtown for Santa Cruz's modern center of economic and cultural activity. Closer to Viru Viru International Airport, the largest airport in Bolivia, the entire El Centro Nuevo development was being managed by Sine Qua Non International. Roberto Gonzalez, its vice president for Western Hemisphere Operations, was in charge of the project, and had been on site since ground was broken three years earlier.

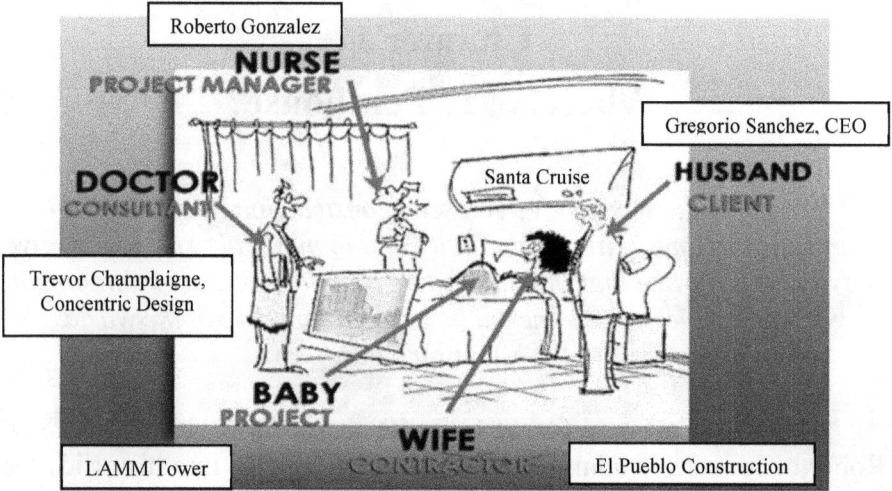

"No, Alessandra, I didn't forget to invite them. I've been in the business a long time and have seen more than one case in which a client like Mr. Sanchez finds something wrong with the project. It would be embarrassing for our entire team and everyone in Sine Qua Non if that were to appear on the evening news not only here in Bolivia but all over South America. We're better off greeting him with our own senior team and the deputy mayor for Construction and Commerce. Later on, if all goes well, we can have a formal ribbon-cutting ceremony with the mayor, the president of Bolivia, and even the Pope if he wants to come. Today will be a more private affair." Roberto Gonzalez had managed international projects the size of El Centro Nuevo before and was talking from experience. Besides, he had developed a kind of sixth sense for spotting difficult clients, and Gregorio Sanchez had convinced him early on that something unexpected might happen. He was strangely absent from many of the meetings he should have attended as the building went up, although his representatives had been paying attention to all the details and hadn't done anything particularly unusual so far. Still, for the man writing the checks for construction of the tallest building in Bolivia, it was odd for him to be making his first appearance in La Paz to inspect the building when it was topped off.

"Okay, Mr. Gonzalez, I just wanted to be sure this wasn't something I needed to take care of before Mr. Sanchez arrives tomorrow morning. He'll be arriving in his corporate helicopter; it's a good thing we completed the helipad on time so he can use it. But it's only a short drive from Viru Viru; Mr. Sanchez seems like he enjoys making a spectacle of himself," Alessandra replied.

"Thanks, Alessandra," Roberto Gonzalez said. "Let's call all the project team members together for a last run-through before our big day."

"They're already in the conference room. They're pretty excited. You can go in whenever you're ready," she said. "I'm on my way right now."

Roberto followed her out of his office and down the hall to the conference room. The project team's headquarters were located in one of the site's first completed structures, which would one day be used by the real estate management company that would lease space to corporate and residential occupants. It was a beautiful building inside and out, with a similar gleaming glass façade designed to mirror the LAMM Tower for pedestrians as they stroll through the landscaped park that was the centerpiece of El Centro Nuevo.

"So, everyone, are we all ready for tomorrow?" Roberto asked as he convened the meeting. Present were members of El Pueblo Construction and all their subcontractors; Concentric Design, the architectural firm from London that had designed the entire development; and of course the local representatives of LAMM. Except for LAMM, the most senior staff of all the other companies were on hand for the big occasion, and had been for several days.

"Yes, we're ready and happy to be here," said Trevor Champlaigne, the senior architect from Concentric Design who had surprised everyone except for Roberto Gonzalez when he flew in to see his baby when its sub and superstructures were completed. "I never miss a moment like this." He had brought four of his trusted assistants with him, and they were all pompously present, thanking Alessandra profusely for honoring their request for English tea instead of Bolivia's finest coffee at the meeting.

The contractors were represented by the president of El Pueblo and all seven of his subcontractor companies, plus the heads of four different construction unions representing the hundreds of workers who had been working since day one. Even the LAMM representatives were visibly excited, since the letters "LAMM" would one day be shining from all four sides of the top of the tower, some thirty-five stories higher than the next-tallest building in the city. Everyone was ready for a quick review of the day's planned agenda, even though it was an "unofficial" visit without dignitaries or the press.

"I want to thank all of you for your good work in completing this phase of the project on time and under budget," Roberto began. "We still have a great deal of work to do on the interior, of course, not to mention much of the entire El Centro Nuevo site. But tomorrow we'll be giving the client their first in-person look at the centerpiece, so I want to be sure we've left nothing to chance. Does anyone have any questions or concerns?"

No one did, of course. Roberto Gonzalez was the best in the business, and he had run this project in the most professional way possible. He prescribed to the "there are no such things as problems, only issues to solve" method of project management, and had encouraged all members of his team to come forward with concerns in an open and nonjudgmental way throughout the three years of construction. There were issues, of course, like the time when the deputy mayor for Construction and Commerce raised concerns about wayfinding signage being in three languages, adding French to the specified Spanish and English, after which one of the unions, which also did substantial work in Brazil, voiced their concern that if a third language were to be added it should be Portuguese. This minor fracas took a few weeks to resolve, which Roberto did with his usual grace and efficiency by appealing to his connections with the Bolivian government in La Paz, where signage was essentially 100 percent Spanish, to keep to the specified English and Spanish languages, and no more. Even a politician with an ego the size of the mayor of Santa Cruz was not about to insist on adding French when he was called to a meeting with the president of Bolivia. Roberto Gonzalez knew how to call in a favor.

"So tomorrow is May 18, and we're actually about two weeks ahead of our target date of June 1 for completion of the tower. I'm proud of all of you and look forward to a nice visit with Mr. Sanchez and his staff tomorrow morning. His helicopter will arrive around 9:00 AM, and I'd like no more than two representatives from each of our team members to be present to greet him. We'll shake hands and I'll show everyone to the cars for our short drive to the front doors of his new tower, where we'll gather for brief remarks by him and him alone. I'll thank him and introduce him but won't say anything else. This is an informal presentation and tour, so our focus will be on leading him around and through the building, hardhats of course. We'll take one of the completed elevators to the top so he can see the view, and point out where most of the key interior features will be once they're completed. The whole tour should take no more than two hours, and will be followed by a lunch here in the conference room. Then he and his team will fly back to the airport and we'll convene again to follow up with our impressions of his visit and what, if anything, we might need to adjust based on his comments. But you've all been through these sorts of things before; I don't need to tell you what to expect. Again, any questions before we finish up our afternoons?"

"Do you think he might want to stay for this evening's football match?" Hernan Cordoba, one of the union representatives, had the only question. "I can arrange for tickets if he and his staff want to attend. It's going to be quite a game; our Club Oriente Petrolero is playing the Club Destroyers from La Paz."

"That's a nice idea and I'd suggest you make the invitation, Hernan," Roberto answered. "But I can tell you that Mr. Sanchez is a fairly private man and he's already told us he would like to leave in the early afternoon. Still, nothing like showing a little hospitality from the city where his company name will soon be visible in lights from everywhere. Although I expect the best part of his visit will be his first look at his new building."

With no more questions, Roberto adjourned the meeting and everyone went back to wrap up their afternoons; they were all looking forward to a successful morning visit from the president of their client company.

*   *   *   *   *   *

May 18 dawned bright and mild. It was late autumn in Santa Cruz but the temperature was still in the mid sixties and wouldn't get much colder. Roberto Gonzalez and his team were all on site by 8:00 AM, making final preparations for Mr. Sanchez's visit and checking whether all was in order in and around the tower. Roberto was a bit nervous, as he always was on mornings like this, but he was also confident that his team was well prepared and the building was looking good for its first performance, even if it was an informal one. Alessandra was early of course, and was already in touch with LAMM to make sure Mr. Sanchez was on schedule. He would arrive at Viru Viru in a private jet at 9:00 AM and would board his helicopter for the short flight to the helipad at El Centro Nuevo to arrive no later than 10:00 AM as scheduled.

"We're all set. Everyone is here; each of the teams kept to their two-person limit except for LAMM. They insist that four of them be there when Mr. Sanchez lands and I told them I'd ask you for permission," Alessandra said.

"Yes, of course, that's what I expected," Roberto said. With that, he and everyone on his team made themselves as busy as they could while they waited to head over to the helipad at 9:45.

The helicopter arrived precisely at 10:00 AM, and Gregorio Sanchez, president of Latin American Mining and Metals, stepped out to greet the project team, along with his personal assistant. This was a bit of a surprise, since plans were for four vice presidents from LAMM headquarters in Santiago de Chile to accompany him, representing finance, strategic planning, corporate relations, and marketing. This was news to Alessandra, who had confirmed a party of six only an hour earlier that morning. Further, Mr. Sanchez seemed oddly distant, with a noticeable lack of enthusiasm for his visit to Santa Cruz, particularly in light of the high spirits of Roberto Gonzalez's project team. After brief handshakes with all eight team members, they got into their cars and drove to the front door of the LAMM Tower.

The deputy mayor and union representatives had arranged for valets and doormen to be present, which was odd for the occasion but was something Roberto Gonzalez decided not to fight. He thought the formalities of opening car doors for a group of ten—not sixteen—official visitors were funny, particularly because eight of whom had been on site nearly every day for three years. They were followed by the even funnier welcoming gestures of the doormen stationed at the still-unfinished entry to the building, which included the presentation of hardhats everyone was required to wear for the duration of the tour. Several project team members tried to hide their own laughter, but not Mr. Sanchez or his assistant.

The group walked around the exterior of the building first, with Roberto as official tour guide. Members of his team chimed in to add color and context to key details—the British architects describing the unique reflecting glass that would be used in the building's exterior, for example. Its insulating qualities would add functionality to the windows' blue tint, which was designed as homage to Bolivian Blue Sodalite, the marble stone native to the country that was also planned for the building's interior finishes and lobby floor. At one point in the tour, they walked across the El Centro Nuevo development's central landscaped park, nearly all the way to the building used by the project team, to get a better view of the tower itself. Gregorio Sanchez said absolutely nothing during the tour, except for a noticeable grunt when Roberto pointed out the top of the tower, noting how it creates a new central point for the Santa Cruz skyline.

The project team grew more concerned as the tour continued inside the tower, up one of the construction elevators, stopping at the twentieth and fortieth floors for brief views of the locations for office space on the lower floors and hotel and residential suites on the upper levels. El Pueblo Construction had even created a few presentation boards of these interior spaces to give Mr. Sanchez a better feel for how his building would function when it was occupied. Still he said nothing, other than asking if he could make a private call to headquarters on his cell phone from the fortieth floor. Of course, the team accommodated his request and stood by making awkward small talk with his assistant while he was gone for a good 15 minutes. He returned, said nothing other than expressing his interest in continuing

7

with the tour, and they all got into the elevator for the tour's final stop, the sixtieth and top floor of the tower.

They arrived to a beautiful view in a space that was still unfinished, except for a large table with design drawings for the restaurant and observation deck that would one day grace the top of LAMM Tower. Alessandra had arranged this as a place for informal discussions with Mr. Sanchez for a few minutes at the conclusion of the tour and had even arranged for hot and cold drinks, before they headed back down for the more formal lunch meeting in their offices. Since the building was still a skeleton, they didn't want to stay too long at the top, given the cool morning temperatures and the risk of windy conditions while they were visiting the tower's interior floors. As it turned out, it wasn't particularly windy on May 18, something the project team had assumed was a sign of good luck.

It wasn't.

When the team returned to the ground level and as they prepared to get into their cars for the drive back to the Sine Qua Non conference room for lunch, Mr. Sanchez turned to Roberto Gonzalez and spoke for the first time all morning.

"Where is my penthouse?" he asked. "You were supposed to build a private penthouse for me on the two top floors of the tower and it's not there. How could you guys not have thought about that? I want that penthouse, and you'll have to increase the building by two floors before I approve any more construction."

Roberto Gonzalez was shocked, as were every other member of his team, but he kept silent. The architects, however, did not.

"Why, we knew of no such requirement," Trevor Champlaigne blurted out. "That's never been mentioned before in any of our meetings with Latin American Mining and Metals, neither in person nor in written correspondence. I'm quite sure of it."

"Well, Mr. Champlaigne, I'm the owner of this tower and I can assure you that we in fact require nothing less than a two-story penthouse on the top of our tower here in Santa Cruz," he said to the architect, staring at him coldly. "With a private elevator, of course." Trevor Champlaigne had no reply.

8

Of course, other than a few gasps and "buts," no one else on the team had anything to say either. They all looked at Roberto Gonzalez to push back at the client, who had obviously made an abrupt new demand that no one had even anticipated until the moment he spoke about his missing penthouse.

"I'm sorry, Mr. Sanchez, but I've never been aware of that requirement," Roberto said, maintaining as professional as he possibly could under the circumstances. "I promise we'll look into the matter and get back to you as soon as we can."

Roberto knew the issues he would need to solve would be many and complex. There would be zoning requirements with the city of Santa Cruz, reworking of load calculations for the building's foundation and structural beams, and changes in electrical and mechanical systems, to say nothing of the new private elevator. It would be a huge undertaking, one that would take months and a great deal of money to solve. Still, he knew from experience that this was no place to have an argument.

Mr. Sanchez continued his shocking pronouncement. "I expect you will get back to me with an answer, and sooner rather than later. Forgetting a detail like this is inexcusable. I will await your reply in my headquarters office in Santiago and until then, I will authorize no further progress on LAMM Tower. I will also speak with my counterparts at Sine Qua Non headquarters and will seek their assurances that nothing proceeds with the El Centro Nuevo project that might interfere with the immediate remedy of this serious error. And since there is nothing else for us to discuss, I will be leaving here immediately. You can contact me through my assistant. But remember, I want that two-story penthouse added to the building, and if you can't do that, Latin American Mining and Metals will find a project management team that will. Good day. May we please make arrangements to take one of your cars back to our helicopter so we can depart?"

And with that, he and his assistant walked toward the first of the waiting cars. Roberto Gonzalez followed him alone and spoke to the driver, telling him to do as Mr. Sanchez had said. The car drove off, leaving the project team in a state of shock.

"All right, everyone, let's go back to the conference room. We have some serious planning to do, and we need to start right now," Roberto Gonzalez said.

At the conference table, there was substantially more conversation than anyone dared in the presence of Gregorio Sanchez. In fact, it bordered on bedlam.

"This is an outrage!" Trevor Champlaigne shouted. "That man has no right to make such a design demand once a building is structurally complete. What could he possibly be thinking? Adding two additional floors will completely ruin the aesthetics! If it were up to me, I would sue him for some sort of breach of contract."

"Do you have any idea of how much reworking of all the systems will be required?" asked the head of El Pueblo Construction. "I mean the load requirements are a nightmare, and I have no idea how to add a private elevator at this point without tearing through all sorts of finished construction."

The only people more circumspect than Roberto Gonzalez were the on-site representatives of LAMM. They were in the most awkward position of anyone, since they knew Mr. Sanchez had never mentioned this requirement to any of them before this morning. They couldn't criticize their boss, but they weren't going to risk their jobs by siding with the rest of the project team. Their silence was deafening even if a few team members had some sympathy for them.

Roberto Gonzalez took control of the meeting in a way that only he could. "We all know this is ultimately something far beyond our control. I will check all the communication logs to make doubly sure there was no mention of a two-story penthouse or a sixty-two-story building in any of our design documents or meetings of any kind with anybody from LAMM. But even if we find a way to prove that we're correct, the client is the client, and this is a very important project for all of us and for the City of Santa Cruz de la Sierra. We'll eventually have no choice but do as Mr. Sanchez says, and I'll be damned if I want to sit here and watch some new project team come in and mess up the project we've been working on for three years. There's a lot to solve and rework, but the building is still a skeleton, and that means there are still a lot of possible solutions. I suggest we all have our lunch, take a deep breath, and adjourn to tackle the issues we think are most important from our perspective. Then, starting tomorrow, we'll get on with the business of adding that penthouse in a way that works best for all of us, including Mr. Sanchez. I say we gather here at 9:00 AM to start the process. Now, let's eat."

"Well, at least we don't have to sit through tonight's game with that turkey," said Hernan Cordoba. "Anybody want tickets?"

*   *   *   *   *   *

What happened to Roberto Sanchez and his team? Why did Gregorio Sanchez invent a crisis during the construction of such a large building in such an important project in Bolivia's largest city without the hint of a warning? How could no one have seen this coming? What was behind this most irrational development in a project headed by someone as impeccably qualified and experienced as Roberto Gonzalez?

What the project team failed to understand, because it was not revealed to them and could never be revealed to them, was that the issue was not the fact that the client wanted to add two more stories to LAMM Tower at such a late stage in its construction. The client had no interest in that building, and wasn't merely acting in an irresponsible and capricious way. The client wasn't stupid, as some members of the team thought. In fact, the client was acting in a completely rational way that advanced his own self-interest.

He was causing a dramatic delay in the project schedule and an enormous increase in the project budget because for him, these were not failures at all. They were justifications for the project's true goals, which were to create a stable and long-lasting financial operation that would allow for the unrecorded flow of funds from the client to a project that had nothing to do with the tallest building in Bolivia, or the new commercial and civic center of Santa Cruz de la Paz. The client was in fact really working for the Chilean government, and the money that was officially part of the budget for the LAMM Tower and El Centro Nuevo was being sent in secret to the military establishment of Venezuela to fund its shipment of weapons to the Colombian

11

government for its operations against the Revolutionary Armed Forces of Colombia (FARC). The client would succeed in achieving these goals as long as the LAMM Tower project schedule continued beyond its advertised completion date, and as long as large new sums of money were passing through its "official" budget to fund the secret military mission the client was sponsoring.

No one on Roberto Gonzalez's team could be expected to know anything about this, although Roberto himself may have suspected something was amiss given the way his client had been acting throughout the first three years of the LAMM Tower project. It's important to remember that in this case, what appears to be a legitimate commercial development project—a sixty-story office and residential tower in the middle of a huge urban development program—is not at all what it appears. It is in fact a political project, designed to allow for huge sums of money to pass through what seem to be legitimate purchases of materials and services but are in fact transfers of money disguised as these types of expenditures when they are actually financial support for cross-border military operations in countries that have nothing to do with the project's official goals.

Progress toward the completion of LAMM Tower can continue, of course, and it will likely be completed, because the client does not want to draw attention to the possibility of the real purpose by leaving behind an empty El Centro Nuevo development or an incomplete sixty-story tower. It will just take a lot longer and cost a lot more money. It will end not with the completion of a sixty-story building, but with the conclusion of the military operations in Colombia—if they are ever completed. Eventually, if it is necessary to disguise the continued flow of money to support Colombia's fight against FARC, the LAMM Tower will be completed and a new project will be initiated somewhere else in another city in another country to continue the flow. But on the other hand, if the need for continued financial support for Colombia's struggle against FARC should end before the completion of the LAMM Tower, the construction of the tower will also cease, or will continue on the most limited budget possible.

Roberto Gonzalez's team is a fictional one of course, as is every element of this story except for the real city of Santa Cruz de la Sierra, its Viru Viru International Airport and the Club Oriente Petrolero and Club Destroyers football teams. Still, the story illustrates one of many possible ways a corrupt and incompetent project can mask the true destination of the money that flows through it on the way to a purpose that is unknown to project team members or even the client representatives on site. This book will describe ways in which project managers can spot these types of projects in their real-life experiences, and find ways to manage them that will lead to success on site and in their careers. It will also look at some of the larger design issues associated with political projects that are perhaps more visible in their overall goals but still flawed in their replacement of real design and planning considerations—things like the connections between people that make buildings and development projects and even cities and countries succeed and thrive—with political objectives that divide people and restrict them in ways that allow them to be exploited for other purposes.

Chapter 2
What It Means When All Is Not as It Seems

*"Contracting corruption has been around since the construction
of the Appian Way."*
~ Matt Taibbi, American Author and Journalist

Our story of Roberto Gonzalez and his team in Santa Cruz de la Sierra is less fictionalized than readers may think, as are the experience and skills our fictional project manager applied to keep his team motivated and on track to see to the successful completion of the suddenly taller LAMM Tower. It was not an ideal situation, and it could have been worse. This chapter will introduce some of the techniques a manager can use to analyze a project and determine whether a parallel political or corrupt agenda is part of the reality that must be understood, even if it can never be fully managed. In other words, if you as the project manager, or "nurse" in our delivery room analogy, are in fact helping to deliver twins, you can still learn ways to determine whether this is true. If it is, you then have the choice: you can do your best to deliver the twin for which you are responsible—the project you were hired to manage—while leaving the second, secret one in the able care of the stakeholders you will never know. Or, if you prefer, you can resign from the project because it violates your personal ethical standards, with at least the knowledge you have a defensible reason for doing so. (There is a third option, which we have seen and do not recommend to anyone—and that is to remain in charge of the project and join in the corruption, taking advantage of the fact that the client is in fact less interested in the details of your twin than the secret one. We will talk more about team members who make this choice in later chapters.)

The chart below is a starting point for determining whether you are working in a project that may have a secret political or corrupt agenda. The vertical axis includes ten standard elements of any large construction or development project, while the horizontal axis distinguishes how these elements appear or behave in a "normal" vs. a political or corrupt project.

	Normal Projects	Political Projects
Integration	Well Integrated	No Integration
Scope	Well Identified	Hidden Scope
Time		
Cost		
Quality		
Human Resources	Logical and able to Plan, Excecute, Monitor and Control and Close	Unlogical and Difficult to Plan, Excecute, Monitor and Control and Close.
Communication		
Risk		
Procuremet		
Stake Holders	Well Identified	Unknown

In a "standard" project, all parties essentially understand and agree on the ten ways to measure and track a project's successful progress, while in a "political" project, the client (or the client's secret stakeholder) has its own confidential criteria for measuring the success of the project—one that is different—and also hidden—from the other members of the project team.

In political projects, three of the key characters of the project team—the project manager/nurse, contractor/mother, and the designer/doctor—can be seen to be progressing "normally" in translating design documents into physical buildings and support systems, planning work schedules and budgets and tracking progress against them, and in assembling the large teams of construction workers, supply chains, project management specialists, and quality control systems that are familiar to anyone who has worked on a large construction or development project.

The difference in political projects lies in the fact that the client/father—the fourth of four project team members—has a very different agenda, one that is completely different from the stated goal of the project and the ten ways in which the "normal" project's success will be measured. This difference will remain throughout all project phases and at various times—when the project must be adjusted to fit the client's secret agenda—will create chaos and confusion when the project team is ordered to make changes based on the client's secret agenda. Chaos and confusion result from the fact that the changes ordered by the client will likely be a complete surprise, and will have no bearing on agreed-on plans and the execution of those plans up to the point of the client's surprise change of direction.

But since the client controls the overall project's management direction and is the ultimate arbiter of its success or failure, these sudden changes will prevail and the other project team members will be forced to either adapt to them, resign from the project, or be fired in disgrace for failure to perform, or—as discussed earlier—join in the fun of taking advantage of the opportunities for personal gain. The project will then continue with a team that is composed of members who are new to the job, or who are resigned to the fact that their client is marching to the beat of its own drum.

This will continue for another period in which agreed-on construction documents, project schedules, budgets, and quality standards are once again in place—only this time, they will be based on the new project characteristics that follow the client's surprising and confusing definition of success. Things will move forward in another period of relative normalcy, one that may be long or short, until the next moment when the client once again surprises everyone with new and similarly confusing changes, causing another round of adaptation on the fly, shuffling of project management personnel, and new documents, schedules, and budgets.

This new round of changes will come and go in ways similar to previous ones, and in all likelihood it won't be the last. The project will continue for as long as it serves the client's secret agenda, and will end when the goals included in that agenda are achieved or are no longer important to the client. When the project ends, it will do so based on the client's secret agenda and timetable, so that members of the project team and the public at large will likely see an incomplete or "failed" construction site with unoccupied or unfinished buildings, inadequate infrastructure, and perhaps the complete abandonment of the site followed by vandalism, decay, and demolition.

Project managers who are either on site when the project is halted or have come and gone long before will be left to explain to themselves—and worse, to future clients and collaborators—why the project failed. In many cases, they will carry the blame for that failure into the next stages of their careers. They will try to explain what happened based on experiences and project management concepts from other times that they think are relevant. The budget wasn't adequate to achieve quality standards; the development was based on faulty marketing research or fell victim to changing demographics between the time it was conceived and construction began; the client's company was sold to a larger corporation with different business interests; or new government environmental and/or quality standards were imposed in mid-project, creating barriers to completion that were too expensive to overcome.

But none of these explanations will be the truth. The real reason will be that the client has its own secret project goals that no one else knows. The project will continue as long as progress toward these goals is being achieved. Every other member of the project team will be working toward the project's stated or public goals, which will be fine for the client as well—at least as long as they do not conflict with or obstruct progress toward what the client ultimately wants to achieve.

*　*　*　*　*　*

Readers may be confused by these abstract definitions of what is actually happening in a construction or development project that is ruled by political goals that are different from the its stated goals. This confusion is at least partly intentional, as is our use of fictionalized case studies, so we can simulate the same sense of unease or even fear that occurs among project teams working under these conditions. Our review of the ten project measurement standards will probably not bring a sense of stability or normalcy; in fact, the resulting knowledge or understanding of the true nature of a corrupt or political project will be far from comforting. But it will at least explain the reasons behind similar and very real projects that are underway throughout the world right now. And since we believe there are no problems other than events that are fatal to the continued progress on a construction site, our goal in writing this book is to help project managers solve these issues in the best way possible. Step one in solving any issue is arriving at an accurate understanding of it, and that is our objective in writing this book.

Our story of the LAMM Tower in Chapter One begins with the selection of a project manager to bring the project to life; after being awarded the scope of work, the manager is given construction documents describing the work to be done, along with specifications for quality (perhaps several of the retail spaces will be fitted with marble and fine wood, or there will be extensive indoor and outdoor landscaping work in keeping with the project's identity as a "luxury" destination). The project's budget and schedule will also be provided in detail, so the manager can build the team necessary to complete the work according to its specifications, materials can be sourced, and progress can be measured.

In short, everything appears to be consistent with the stated goal of developing a luxury mixed-use urban center, one that will be a showcase of the country's emerging economic success and its plans for serving a growing population with increasing wealth and the choices wealth brings.

However, the client in this case has very different goals. Its interest is to fund a neighboring country's military establishment with funding necessary to support clandestine operations in a third (and rival) nation's civil war. The LAMM Tower exists for no other purpose than to provide a mechanism for unrecorded financial transactions disguised as the costs required to build it.

The consequences of the client's real goal for the project are profound. Readers may jump to the conclusion that there are really two goals for the project, and that they coexist in the client's mind. But in fact the client only has one goal—to provide secret funding for another country's military. The LAMM Tower is merely a means toward that end; the client doesn't care about its success or failure in achieving the public goal of creating a new destination for residents and tourists. It will tolerate successful progress as long as that progress serves its single goal of funneling money to its military partner, but if for any reason the flow of money required by that partner is jeopardized or interrupted, the client will do whatever is necessary to maintain or increase the amount of money required to achieve its real purpose.

Events that might affect the flow of money that is the project's single real purpose may or may not be related to the construction of the tower itself. They may in fact happen in other countries beyond the border of the nation where the mall is under development. Perhaps the dynamics of the civil war in the third country have changed, requiring more (or less) financial support than initially intended. Or the second country's government has changed its priorities and funding operations in a third country is no longer a priority. There are any number of other issues that may arise that will motivate the client to change the luxury mall project's resources, management standards, or measurement factors.

However, when these developments require changes in the LAMM Tower project, those changes will be demanded by the client and the project team will have no choice other than to make them as required. Individual team members can leave the project through resignation or termination, but there are only two choices: go along with the client's sudden new priorities or leave the team. This choice can be rendered impossible, of course, if the client's decision is to terminate the project in its entirety, as has happened on a number of occasions. In this case, the only option is to stop work.

The client may communicate changes in the project in any way they see fit. They may inform the project manager that one of the buildings on the site is not built to their original specifications, even if this is not true, as was the case for Roberto Gonzalez in Chapter One.

The client may also claim that a major structure is located in the wrong place and needs to be demolished and reconstructed in its "proper" location. They may "discover" that the fits and finishes in the project's interior areas are not consistent with their requirements and need to be removed and replaced. They may do anything they want, and it may be true that the specifications they cite as being violated did not exist or were unknown to the other members of the project team but it won't matter: they are the client, and their requirements must be followed.

Looking at another example, we can imagine the fact that there is something else behind a fictional United States president's interest in building a wall along the border between the United States and Mexico. What if the "real" purpose of this wall—specified by a theoretical administration and not the current president—were to funnel money allocated to the wall to another secret project, or perhaps were to build a wall that could be breached by digging tunnels below it despite its stated goal of being impossible? In either of these cases, the government agency managing the project for the administration wouldn't care about the quality of the wall's construction or its materials, or even if the project were completed on the stated schedule. As long as the money is flowing to the other secret project, or as long as the tunnels or other ways of getting past the wall are being developed, the project will continue. It can be extended beyond the time estimated in the original schedule, or it can be closed early. But in either case, the point is that the real project goals of the client—in this case, a fictional American presidential administration—are different from the ones being followed by the project team that was awarded the contract to construct the wall. Note that Chapter Five includes a broader exploration of the potential assumptions and motivations behind construction of a border wall in the world as it exists today, and as it has existed in past decades and even centuries.

*   *   *   *   *   *

Let's return to a review of each of the ten project measurement standards as they appear at the beginning of this chapter, beginning with the vertical axis of the matrix. We will skip the "integration" standard, since it is in reality the compilation of the other nine. In each of these ten categories, project managers will come to identify inconsistencies between a new "political" project's measurement standards and those more typically found in a "normal" construction or development project.

Ultimately, the purpose of our book is to help project managers succeed and create other value in a project—value that is related to the project's stated and public goals. Because if the client has only one agenda, and that is to achieve goals that are secret and unknown to everyone else, they will almost certainly create a vacuum in leadership on site. The project manager, in a sense, is free to operate in a way that achieves as much success as possible, as long as the risks are within acceptable limits and enough resources remain in place to fund that success. We will discuss these opportunities in more detail later, but suffice it to say that in most political projects, the client is interested in the project appearing to be a success, since any attention drawn to issues or difficulties on the project might lead to further exploration by government officials or the press, increasing the likelihood that the true nature of the project might be exposed. Ironically, it is in the client's interest for the project to succeed, even if their only interest is to mask their true intentions.

1. Scope

Note: The sketches in this chapter are from *ABC-MAnagemENT*, a new book by Yasser and Yara Osman, which introduces the career of international construction and development project management to younger elementary school readers.

The client will adjust the scope of the stated project (the LAMM Tower or the border wall) in order to justify its continued operation or its early termination. Once a political project has been initiated, it serves the client's secret goals—the unrecorded flows of funds are in place, or the other operations supported by these funds are underway. Closing one project and opening a new one to achieve the same secret goals is normally more difficult than simply finding a way to continue the one that is already in place. Adjustments in scope that are inexplicable are a sign that a seemingly normal project is in fact political in nature.

It can often be true that even the client's on-site representatives don't know the real hidden agenda. It is only revealed when the real client shows up and says something like, "Who said we should have put this building over here? Take it down!" Or, "This building is in the wrong place; it needs to be moved over there."

Project team members will sometimes blame such changes on the client being inexperienced or frivolous, or "so rich that they don't care about the cost" and are always ready to waste money as their desires change. But in fact, when it comes to these sudden changes in scope, the secret stakeholder(s)—the real client(s) of a corrupt or political project—know exactly what they are doing.

2. Schedule (Time)

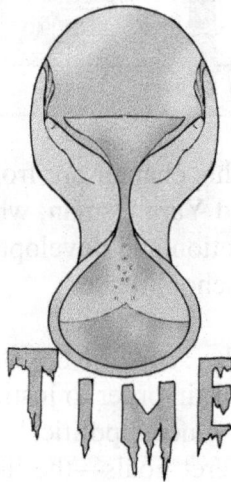

The time allocated for the project—from initiation to closing—will not be consistent with the time normally required for construction to be completed. This is because the operation the project is supporting—providing unrecorded transfers of money to a neighboring country's military operations—has its own schedule. It will have a starting point, and can move through phases consistent with those of a standard construction project. But at some point, because the need for these funds by the second country's military, or the construction of a corrupt official's villa, or the continuing illegal transfer of funds by the project's secret stakeholders(s) will last beyond the project's stated schedule, the project will simply continue. The client's reasons for continuing the project schedule may or may not be work-related; they may, for example, be the need to demolish and relocate a major portion of already-completed construction. Or they may have no explanation at all. But the real reason behind repeated extensions of the schedule will be the fact that the political or corrupt project's secret goals still need to be achieved, on their own schedule. Conversely, a sudden termination of the project can be due to the fact that the secret flow of money is no longer needed, for whatever reason.

In political projects, one of the most important variables is the schedule—as long as there is a need to continue pursuing secret goals, the stated project will continue, and therefore its schedule will be extended or terminated in a way that is unrelated to progress toward official project goals and objectives.

3. Cost

Irregularities in the project's overall budget are the most obvious clue that a project is in fact more political than "real," and is serving a secret purpose. If the total budget is larger than those for similar projects by a factor of two or three or more, it is likely that there are goals beyond the stated construction of a new tower, or a wall, or something else.

But there are other financial clues that can indicate a project is in fact political in nature. One example can be a strange variance in the individual cost estimates making up the overall budget. Some elements will be far more expensive than market prices—for example, door and window frames may be priced several times higher than what can be purchased from local suppliers. But others will be either consistent with market prices or possibly lower— bathroom fixtures or electrical wiring, for example. The reason for these changes may be their use in "justifying" future cost overruns. In this example, the project will suddenly need more (or new) door and window frames in large quantities. The original cost estimates for these components won't change with the new quantities ordered; they will simply be extended by the number of new units ordered, and the total budget will be increased accordingly. On the other hand, in our example, there will likely be few changes in the required number of bathroom fixtures or amount of electrical wiring.

A third sign that a project might be political is a difference in the schedule of progress payments. "Normal" projects often call for a 10 percent advance payment, followed by regular progress payments based on completion milestones, and a final retention of another 10 percent of the total budget (5 percent to be paid on completion, and a final 5 percent to be paid one year later). A political project, on the other hand, might begin with an unusually large initiation fee, perhaps as high as 35 percent. This would allow for the funneling of significant amounts of money toward the project's secret goals—i.e. the neighboring country's military operations, or illegal investments in the stock market

4. Quality

This measurement factor is extremely troublesome because it is obviously inconsistent with the technical expertise of project management teams, and is an early indicator that the client doesn't care about the skills or talent of team members. An analogy of this type of issue is the purchase of a watch. If a person wants a good functional watch to wear every day, and that person is engaged in manual labor, for example, spending money on a durable watch that is comfortable to wear and slim enough to avoid "catching" on things that are carried or manipulated during a workday would be the sensible thing to do. But if the client in this case specifies a high quality Rolex with a fashion watchband, his action wouldn't make sense. When project team members wonder why the client makes such decisions and these questions are not answered, competent team members may simply get fed up. They change from committed team members to collaborators who are no longer committed to the project. They will learn that quality is not an issue, and the smarter ones will learn that they can become corrupt without fear of being caught. In other words, they can also specify ultrahigh quality materials and components, purchase inferior ones at a lower price, and pocket the difference. Relaxed quality standards in political projects lead smart people with diminished ethics to join in the game of padding the project budget, spending less than the budget, and keeping the difference for themselves. This may be an unintended consequence of a client with a secret agenda, but with no oversight, it can become a large component of a political project's waste, contributing to its failure.

5. Human Resources

Hiring practices are a clue about political projects as well. Normally, at the beginning of a project, all team members—the project manager, the contractor, the design team, and the owner/client—look to hire the most qualified and best people for the job. It's natural to go for the best when success in achieving stated goals is everyone's motivation. But in a political project, the client doesn't need—or even want—people who know what's going on. To the extent that the client has hiring responsibility, they may select people who are too junior, or who have a history of incompetence or corruption. It will be easy for other team members to draw their own conclusions about client representatives in this case. But of course, other team members will have the right to hire their own employees, consultants, and advisors. Examples of how new-individuals may suddenly appear on a project team will occur later, in the next chapter.

One possible personnel-related situation is that a team member becomes wise enough to see the client's hidden agenda, or to at least become convinced that there might be one. That team member may seek answers and ask questions to find out what might be the client's "real" purpose. A client who discovers a team member like this will often call for the individual to be terminated. Another possibility is related to our example of the client "discovering" that a building has been constructed without a key detail (such as a penthouse at the top) and needs to be redesigned and reconstructed at great expense, with serious schedule implications. In this case, someone—most likely a member of the project management team—will be the scapegoat, and will be fired by the client for incompetence, even though the manager did nothing wrong.

Continued turnover based on the client removing staff who know too much or ask too many questions, or by the firing of scapegoats, will have the effect of sowing fear and mistrust among project team members. Because of this, along with the need to replace lost talent among the project team, turnover in a corrupt or political project can be very dangerous to its success.

6. Communication

A project manager can normally control communications among members of a project team based on the way that team is officially organized. Below is a formula that can be used to estimate the number of communication channels a team of any size will require:

$[N \times (N-1)]/2$

This formula can be used, for example, to predict that a project team of four members will require six communication channels:

$[4 \times (4-1)]/2 = [4 \times 3]/2 = 12/2 = 6$

Or, for a team of five people, ten channels are needed:

$[5 \times (5-1)]/2 = [5 \times 4]/2 = 20/2 = 10$

These channels can be documented and managed through delegation of responsibility among team members, and by directing responsible team members to maintain and report their own communications throughout the project. In this way, the senior project manager can review these communications channel reports when issues arise that require study to locate and correct misunderstandings.

However, in the case of a political project, when the client arrives on the site and asks, "Who put the building over there?" there is no way for the project manager to track the issue and correct it, since there would not be any record of communications anticipating the issue before the client announced it. If the client had discussed any prior concern with their representative on site, that representative would have been responsible for communicating that concern with someone else on the team, and a concern like the mistaken location of a building would almost surely arise well before the client themselves found it during an official visit.

But since there was no channel for the client to announce this "mistake" (because in fact it is not a project mistake at all but is related to the client's secret goals), there is no opportunity for a project manager to anticipate the issue and make corrections. It is nothing more than a smokescreen to mask the real purpose of announcing a "mistake," which is to extend the project schedule so its secret goal can continue to be achieved on a schedule that is different from the time required for successful completion of construction.

Project managers most often don't know the truth about whether an issue like this is the result of a frivolous client or a client with a hidden political agenda. They only know in their hearts that there was no mistake made by any of their team members, knowledge they can verify by going back and tracking official project communications reports. But they can do little about the issue beyond the choice of following the client's direction or leaving—

that is, unless the client terminates the project manager or closes the project completely.

The purpose of this book is to teach project managers to understand the likely true nature of a project when seemingly unexplained events change or even derail progress toward its stated goals.

One of our most general—and in fact practical—pieces of advice for project managers in these situations is, "Open your mind. You're a good manager. You can see what's going on. Go past your fear and use your understanding of the project's true nature to achieve more."

Instead of being corrupted and pocketing money (see number four, "Quality," above), use resources to focus on the project and its success. Manage to the benefit of the project's stated goals. This can best be achieved by proposing new initiatives to the client. "Let's try this…" can be an effective way to suggest changes. If the client rejects the idea, then it is probably best not to pursue the proposal. But remember that the client may want to say yes for reasons that are not related to the success of the project's stated purpose, but as a way to keep attention away from their real goals. Consistent with our delivery room analogy for corrupt and political projects, "Propose to the client that you want to build healthy twins. If the client wants to take one of them, it's okay. Just ask them to leave you one healthy baby."

7. Risk

In every project, there are always risks. Most of them are manageable, and they become more so as a project manager gains experience. There are three ways to manage risk in a construction or development project: (1) transfer it, for example by buying insurance from a third party; (2) ignore it, because it is probably unlikely to happen; or (3) deal with it by making changes to the project plan. Many project managers develop a risk register that includes these risks and the ways to deal with them.

In a political project, there are risks beyond those included in any assessment or risk register. For example, there is the risk of turnover (see "Human Resources," number five above). This can be destructive to the progress of a particular project, and can also have negative consequences for the career of a team member or even the project manager. Political risks can also be quantified in terms of the additional funds and extended schedule required to demolish and relocate a building.

The problem with the risks involved in political projects is that there is no systematic way to address them. Because the real goal is held in secret by the client, a project manager is likely going to be caught by surprise. For example, what if the government of the third country collapses and there is no longer a need for military operations by the second country in our first example? If this happens six months into a project initially forecast to take two years to complete, the project will end prematurely, leaving an empty or partially-completed construction site.

8. Procurement

This measurement factor offers an interesting a way to anticipate and even assess the true nature of a new project, and to test that assessment early on.

In most cases, the location in which a project is being developed will provide opportunities to maximize the way construction costs are managed. For example, if a new project is being constructed in the Middle East or China, there will be relatively low labor costs, and a resulting higher cost in the procurement of materials. Say a project has a total budget of $350 million. In the Middle East or China, perhaps $240 million of this total will be in procurement of materials, with another $110 million in labor costs. If the project were located in the United States, there might be a division of these expenses that includes higher labor costs—perhaps $175 million in labor and the same $175 million in procurement of materials.

Because labor is almost always salary and wage expense, procurement of materials is an easier way to hide money. "My materials actually cost three times your estimate" is harder to prove wrong than a similar claim about salaries and wages. And in our experience, there are procurement managers who are expert in creating false documentation to support high procurement costs: "If you want corrupt procurement, you always hire a corrupt procurement manager."

One recommendation is to meet with a client's (or contractor's) procurement manager early in the process of initiating a project. In this way, a project manager can tell if the procurement manager is corrupt by using technical information about the materials specified in cost estimates—not by simply looking at the financial numbers alone. Sometimes, entire countries have reputations for corrupt financial dealings in project finances, and it is likely that most or all of the procurement managers in such countries are corrupt. In other cases, there are both ethical and corrupt procurement managers. In both situations, it is important to remember that corrupt people are hired for political projects because they have experience and skill in outsmarting people. They won't reveal they are corrupt, at least not easily.

9. Stakeholders

These are defined as anyone who can assess or affect a project. For example, a bad procurement manager is a bad stakeholder. The client is a stakeholder, as is the designer and the contractor.

In a political project, the real stakeholder is never seen. The client is working for that ultimate stakeholder who might be the prime minister of the country in which the construction project is located, or the leader of a second country that is the destination for money flowing through the secret financial systems that are the project's primary operations. The channels between the stated project—the luxury mall, or the wall—and the ultimate stakeholder can be complicated and hard to discover. But a political project will always operate based on the interests of and decisions made by the ultimate stakeholder.

10. Integration

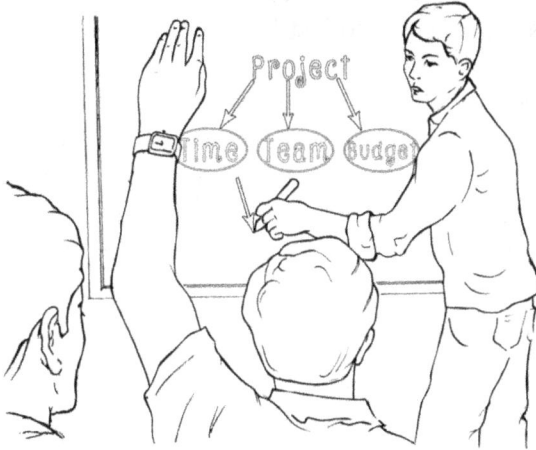

If you were to put the other nine measurement factors into a blender and turn it on to produce a juice, that juice, in a sense, will become what we call the project's overall integration. For a "normal" project, the analogy might be filled out in terms of a specified percentage of ingredients; for example, the juice is X percent strawberry, Y percent banana, and Z percent apple.

However, in a political project, there is no control or understanding of these percentages among the team members on site. The purpose of this chapter is to create a better understanding of the systems and processes of project management so that readers can become better in their careers. Ultimately, taken as a whole, we hope this book explains these same concepts—and how they might be encountered in real life—in a way that increases readers' understanding of the difference between a "standard" construction or development project and a political one.

One significant point to reinforce over and over again is the fact that while everyone wants to finish a real construction project, the client may never want to close a political project, because maintaining a flow of money for its hidden purpose is the client's real goal. Political projects almost always extend beyond the stated schedule for completion, because the flow of money that is their real purpose is intended to last for a long time.

As we close this chapter, we hope it will be easier for readers to understand the projects they are managing in a way that will allow them to realize they might be involved in a political or corrupt project. In the next chapter, we will offer suggestions on what to do with this knowledge.

Chapter 3

Achieving Success in a Political Project—A Guide for Project Managers

"When I bid out our construction projects, I call contractors personally to close the deal and get the best price or enhance the scope of their deliverable. You don't get what you don't ask for."
~ Ivanka Trump

What can project managers do when they suspect they are managing a political or corrupt project? It's human nature to want to know for sure: "Is my project actually funneling money for a secret purpose beyond the construction of a new mixed-use urban development, or international airport, or cruise ship terminal complex?"

In most cases, this is the wrong question for a project manager to ask, because even if we are able to know with certainty that our client is paying for a secret military operation in another country, or circumventing international sanctions against supporting the government in a neighboring country, or even simply trying to funnel money away from the project to invest for profit in the stock market, what can we do about it?

If we confront the client directly with what we know, what will the client do? In most cases, we will almost certainly be looking for another job. If we go to the government or the news media with our knowledge, what will happen then? In the case of a corrupt client who is funneling money into the stock market or skimming profits to buy a yacht or a seaside villa on the Mediterranean, we might find ourselves on the "right" side of our corrupt project and how it is understood by the public, and might be rewarded for preventing this sort of behavior from taking place. But it is also possible that in other cases, the government is aware of and possibly supports our client's secret agenda; in this case, it will do no good to draw their attention to what we think is going on, and in doing so, we might find ourselves in even worse trouble.

The right question for a project manager to ask in these situations is, "How can I best focus on managing what I can control, and does that mean staying with the project to complete it to the best of my abilities, or resigning and moving to a different assignment?"

There are significant risks associated with staying in a project that appears to be one secret stakeholders are using to pursue a scope of work that is equally secret and distinct from the official description of the project being managed. Secret stakeholders can change the project's scope, schedule, budget, quality standards at any time and without warning. They can hire and fire team members based on their own interests, again without any prior notice. This can include the project managers themselves, and may be done in a way that makes them scapegoats for trumped-up "errors" or "mismanagement." In such cases, when project managers find themselves—or worse—their team members—unjustly accused of errors or mismanagement causing a project's scope, schedule, or budget to change, they will normally rely on the ethical standards of project management to be followed. That is, they will expect the charge against the manager or a team member to be backed up with clear evidence or proof of what they are accused of doing. Of course, in a corrupt project there can be no such evidence or clear proof, since the real reasons for the changes are as secret as the stakeholder(s) who are behind them.

But there is also the chance—sometimes a reasonably good chance—that the project as officially described needs to succeed. A secret scope of work might not be secret for long if it gets in trouble in a way that attracts the attention of the local press or government officials who are not part of the secret stakeholder team. A successful ribbon-cutting at the completion of the project is something everyone might want, including the secret stakeholders. And a project manager might even be able to influence things so this eventual successful outcome is more likely. Unless and until something makes this impossible—in other words, when an insoluble problem arises—project managers can consider whether it's best to proceed toward official completion of the project as their best option.

Beyond the possibility that a project's secret stakeholder(s) might in fact support the successful completion of the parts of a project that are under our control, there is also the question of what to do as professionals. We are managers, after all. We use knowledge—technical knowledge about materials, intersecting schedules for construction of various components of our project, the skills, abilities, and even personal qualities of our team members, and any number of other factors—to steer our way to success. Seeking knowledge to explain things when unpredictable events or direction from our clients interrupt our progress is understandable, and in most cases it's the way we solve issues and overcome obstacles. Project managers manage their team, and the team builds the project, so it is our duty as project managers to look after our team members and continue to steer them in a productive and positive direction even in the negative environment of a political or corrupt project.

However, in corrupt or political projects, the knowledge of what our client is doing—or, as is often the case, what our client's client is doing—provides us with no such resources. All we know is that there is a secret agenda; and in our opinion, that is all we need to know. The best thing this knowledge can give us is the understanding that this secret stakeholder is in fact behind the strange things we may be experiencing. In other words, we're not crazy to believe that something beyond our stated project goals is associated with our project, and perhaps more important, that our client is not crazy either. There's an agenda, it's secret, and knowing it won't necessarily help us in any way. But that agenda has a distinct purpose that is rational to the stakeholders who own it; realizing this, we can make our own rational plans to anticipate unpredictable changes in our project's scope, and to maintain steady progress as best as possible.

Managing unpredictable events is part of our profession. If a labor strike happens in mid-schedule, we adapt. If a cyclone makes landfall on our site when partially-completed structures are most vulnerable, we adapt. And when we find ourselves in a project that has a secret political or corrupt agenda, we can adapt as well. In all of these cases, we can't mitigate all risks or prevent all damages. We do the best we can. Focusing on what we can manage is a key professional skill for project managers, and more often than not it leads to success. Distractions that take our attention away from the things we can control increase the risk of failure. The problem we face in corrupt and political projects is the legitimate concern about what else might be happening behind the scenes. Worrying about how a secret agenda might affect our project is worth our time and energy, but only to that extent. It does no one any good to try to become an investigative journalist when our job is to complete a project successfully on the terms we can understand and manage.

It's a morally troubling decision to be sure—after all, doing anything to advance a secret client's secret agenda, particularly when it might involve military operations, or the channeling of resources to enrich a corrupt government or corporation, or even the theft or embezzlement of funds for personal gain ought to be disturbing and difficult. But solving these problems can require power and resources beyond those a single project manager can control.

Deciding to resign from a project when a secret political or corrupt agenda becomes apparent is a reasonable choice in some circumstances, and some may argue that this is the only morally defensible decision a project manager can make. We fully support anyone who chooses this path; this is a personal decision each of us must make as an individual, based on what we believe and how we define our moral compass. As noted in this chapter, and based on the code of ethics that is an essential core of our profession, we disagree to some extent and believe choosing to be a professional project manager brings with it a degree of responsibility for completing the projects we accept. But in a larger sense, we also ask why project managers must tolerate being given such stark and difficult choices. Why must we feel guilty about trying to fulfill a scope of work to the best of our ability because there may be a corrupt or politically objectionable secret agenda associated with it? What if we still believe that the people who live in the city or nation where we are working deserve the best architectural environment we can deliver for them? What if we believe that advancing our careers and providing for our families by applying our skills and experience is more important than most other considerations? What do we do if we discover a secret agenda late in our work and completion is only a short time away?

Are we morally bound to risk everything and resign, or investigate and expose the true nature of our secret client's agenda that is associated with the construction we are managing? Is leaving an incomplete project behind the best way to uphold our moral values? Is allowing a project to limp along to completion without our help and achieving far less than it could have with our continued leadership the right choice? Is risking our careers and perhaps our continued citizenship in the country where we are working a reasonable price we must pay in order to maintain our identity as a professional? One of the main reasons behind our decision to write this book is to open the doors for a discussion of this highly sensitive subject, and to invite colleagues in the field of project management to ask questions we have always struggled to answer. The field of project management to this date still has no licensing requirements or official testing procedures to control who can serve as an official project manager, and there is no governing board in place that is strong enough to protect individual project managers when they face challenges beyond the capacity of a single project manager to address. In reality, any project manager is likely to be exposed to sensitive situations such as a political or corrupt project, or any number of other more common but equally serious risks. In addition to providing some guidance for project managers to use in determining the nature of challenges presented by corrupt or political projects, we also believe the time has come for licensing procedures, certification of the professional capabilities of project managers, and the establishment of a governing board—at least at the national level within the United States—that can protect individual project managers from these risks.

It is our position that as project managers, we should fulfill our responsibilities to the best of our ability. The secret agenda, if it exists, is beyond our control. Completing the project we have been given is, however, something we can control, at least as long as we have the resources and time needed to do our job. In our experience working on projects throughout the world, we have dealt with any number of obstacles in the way of completing a project in a perfect or near-perfect way. Project managers in the United States often find themselves in ideal situations: there are plenty of skilled and experienced project team members who can be assembled to assist in managing various aspects of the work. There are also many skilled and unskilled laborers available to perform the work throughout the project schedule. The latest technology can be brought to the project when necessary to ensure quality, achieve goals for durability, sustainability, and environmental performance. The weather and working conditions may be subject to seasons but are often mild enough to allow work to proceed for large portions of the year. Achieving 95 percent of a project's goals for quality, cost, and schedule is achievable enough to be considered routine.

Even without the presence of a political or corrupt secret agenda, projects in other parts of the world face conditions that are often less than ideal. There can be labor shortages, both skilled and unskilled, for example. Qualified management team members may be hard to find or retain. Budgets may be insufficient to do the job required. And the weather may be too hot or too rainy, or subject to variations that make it difficult to get work done as easily as a project team or client might like. When these obstacles are present, a project manager might find that achieving only 40 percent of the job's quality, cost, and schedule measures is possible without that project manager working extra hard to accomplish more. With that hard work, maybe a project in one of these locations can meet 60 percent of its goals. In our opinion, that additional 20 percent improvement is evidence of solid project management work, and should be acknowledged. Leaving a project to limp along toward a 40 percent level of completion is a sign of nonexistent, or perhaps poor, project management. Even if conditions are difficult enough to prevent reaching more than 60 percent of what a project was intended to achieve, that additional 20 percent is worth the effort. And, in our opinion again, whether those conditions are due to the weather, budget, or labor issues that often plague a "normal" commercial project, or whether they are caused by a secret scope of work that funnels resources away from the project's stated goals. In these cases, when it is clear that achieving 95 percent or even 90 percent of a project's goal cannot be achieved, driving the project to try and achieve such a clearly unrealistic performance standard will in and of itself be a demonstration of failure as a project manager. Realism is an important element in our profession, and we must always adjust our expectations based on our ability to see and understand the reality in which we are operating.

Even with our belief that achieving even limited project goals is the right choice in political or corrupt projects, these are choices we should not be left to make on our own. And it is unfair that we might find ourselves set up to fail in a way that is unpredictable and impossible to anticipate. As we will discuss later in this book and again in the conclusion, there are people and organizations that can help us face challenges like these—challenges that project managers have faced for generations in many parts of the world, and may one day face everywhere. Advocating for powerful institutions that can resist the launch of projects with secret political or corrupt agendas may be the only thing we can do as a community of project managers, given the unequal power balance we face when we try to solve these issues within the confines of a single project. But again, more about this later.

For now we are almost certainly alone, with other members of our team, when we find out that a project we believe is a "normal" commercial development is in fact only the public face of a much larger adventure. The moral decision of what to do is not ours to make; it is one every project manager must do on their own. What we can provide in this book is a way for project managers to better understand the warning signs that a project is not as it seems—ideally earlier than the day a client arrives in a helicopter and asks us why we haven't built his penthouse on top of a sixty-story building.

In the next chapter, we will explore another series of events at a fictional project that is set in the context of a project that is of major historic consequence: the Panama Canal in 1912. With certain historical limitations—travel by steamship and not by air; communication via Transatlantic cable instead of the internet; and international relations involving different global superpowers and regional governments and industries—we will create a kind of historic game, the kind that might make for a good video or board game, to illustrate the ways in which a project manager can identify characteristics of a project that might provide a good warning that there is a secret agenda controlled by secret stakeholders.

While the ways in which this information might become available to a project manager can involve any of the ten project measurement standards outlined in Chapter 2—budget, schedule, human resources, integration, etc.—we will illustrate how they all lead back to two basic standards that are a constant in every corrupt or political project. Those are (1) the scope, and (2) the client or stakeholder(s). A corrupt or political project will always have a secret scope, and it will always have secret stakeholders. Because these fundamental elements of the project will always be unknown to the project manager, they cannot be controlled, and they can disrupt or cause harm to the official project at any time. Still, knowing that they are present allows a project manager to make decisions that can minimize these risks and to create the best possible project under the circumstances should the project team choose to stay and try to finish the job.

And, as we will see in later chapters, this knowledge might one day be used to prevent or restrict the initiation of a corrupt or political project through the establishment of professional standards and for certification of project managers, and an organization that can review and approve projects that can demonstrate that they are free from these secret agenda. But for now, it's on to the city of Colón, on the Atlantic coast of Panama, in 1907, where we are seven years away from the completion of the Panama Canal. We will be managing the construction of a deepwater port to handle commodities and agricultural products shipped through the canal from neighboring Latin American countries, where they will be offloaded for transfer to larger ships taking them across the Atlantic and Pacific Oceans to Europe and Asia, and the relocation of sections of the Panamanian transcontinental railroad that must be moved in order to accommodate the route of the canal.

The Panama Canal's strategic location is largely based on geography: the distance between the Atlantic and Pacific Oceans is only 45 miles.

Chapter 4

How Corruption Might Have Looked Along the Panama Canal in 1907

"My impression about the Panama Canal is that the great revolution it is going to introduce in the trade of the world is in the trade between the east and the west coast of the United States."
~ William Howard Taft, President of the United States 1909–1913

[NOTE: The authors have created this fictional project and set it in the historical context of the Panama Canal in order to illustrate many of the characteristics of secret political and corrupt projects we might encounter in today's world. Placing the story in a time more than a century ago, in a location reasonably close to the southern border of the United States, is intentional. It allows us to introduce characters and situations based on our real-life experience without creating opportunities for readers to try and guess which country or what companies and individuals might be the "true" country or company or individual behind any element of the story. Eliminating this intrigue is not simply a desire to protect real countries or companies or individuals; it is also our way of keeping the readers' focus on the issues we believe are more important for today's project managers, and avoiding distractions that might draw attention away from them.

In order to keep the analogies in our historical fiction relevant to the challenges today's project managers face in corrupt or political projects, certain facts of history are adjusted or ignored entirely. These include the precise details of the deepwater port of Colón, along with its docks, maintenance facilities, and the dates of their construction. Similarly, the relocation of the Panamanian transcontinental railroad is in our story under the authority of the Panamanian government, while in reality it was managed by the United States Isthmian Canal Commission, which controlled the ten-mile-wide zone in which the canal was being constructed and through which much of the railroad was located. Finally, all of the individuals and corporations, with the exception of President Manuel Amador Guerrero, are fictitious, as are the unfairly scandalous stories of him hiring two young Mexicans to divert money from the Colón Deepwater Port Project for construction of his vacation villa on the Pacific Coast of Panama. We sincerely apologize to anyone these storytelling liberties may have offended.]

*   *   *   *   *   *

It's the spring of 1907, and you have just been hired as the project manager for construction of a deepwater port in the city of Colón, Panama, at the mouth of what will soon become one of the most important shipping channels in the world. Construction of the Panama Canal is well underway and is scheduled to open, locks and all, in six and one-half years, at the end of 1913.

Your project is actually a combination of three separate scopes of work, all awarded to a Panamanian construction company on a design-build basis. The three projects are (1) the docks themselves, including dredging to accommodate ships that can sail across the Atlantic Ocean, cranes for loading and offloading the ships, and storage areas where cargo can be held while awaiting transfer to another ship; (2) a ship maintenance and repair facility, including drydocks, machine shops, with a headquarters office building that will house management staff for the entire docking facility; and (3) relocation of sections of the original transcontinental Panamanian railway, originally built in 1855, that connects Colón with Panama City on the Pacific coast. Construction of the canal has required relocation of several sections of this then-important rail link.

The timeframe for completion of your project is the end of December of 1913, nearly seven years from now. The goal is for the port, its maintenance and repair facilities, and the relocated transcontinental railway to be fully operational before the canal opens to international commercial shipping in early 1914. Labor is plentiful, given the large number of workers being hired to work on the canal since construction began in earnest in 1904, which has attracted laborers from all over Panama, Colombia, and other nearby nations. Many of these unskilled laborers needed for construction are eager to work in Colón and along the new rail corridor because it is considered less dangerous and remote than work on the canal itself. Money is also readily available; the port of Colón is a way for Panama to capitalize on the canal and the shipping traffic it will attract, a keen priority for its new government given the relatively minor ongoing revenue it will receive in lease payments for the canal from the United States. Since the 1902 "revolution" that separated Panama from being part of the nation of Colombia, the new country has been dominated by the United States, which supported the revolution, and in turn established a financial arrangement with Panama heavily in the Americans' favor. Port fees, ship repair and maintenance, and taxes on goods brought to the port for shipping overseas will be a significant source of revenue for Panama, in all likelihood more valuable than the annual lease fees coming from the United States.

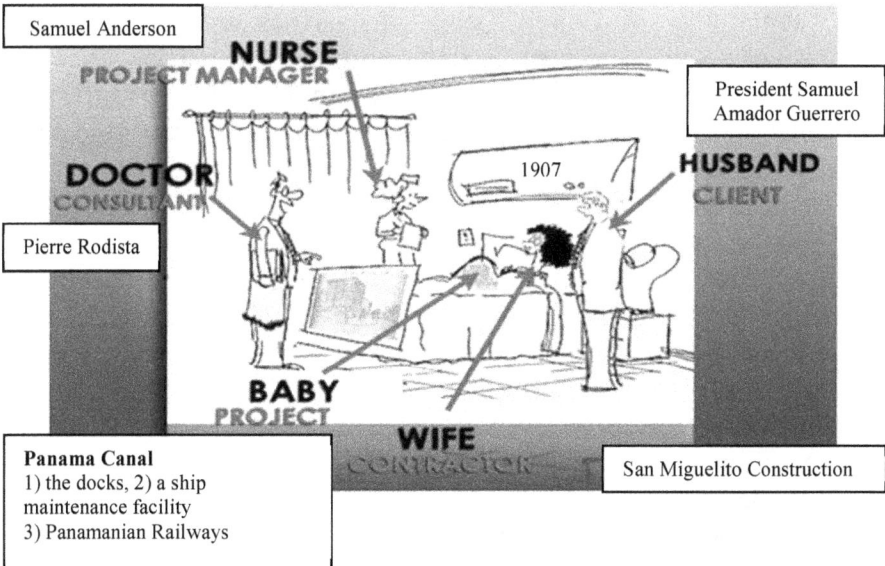

Samuel Anderson

NURSE
PROJECT MANAGER

President Samuel Amador Guerrero

DOCTOR
CONSULTANT

1907

HUSBAND
CLIENT

Pierre Rodista

BABY
PROJECT

WIFE
CONTRACTOR

Panama Canal
1) the docks, 2) a ship maintenance facility
3) Panamanian Railways

San Miguelito Construction

Funding from the Panamanian government is coming from investments by mining and agricultural companies in Colombia, Ecuador, Bolivia, and Chile, who stand to greatly increase their sales to Europe via the completed canal. Similar investments from Costa Rica and Nicaragua are based on their hopes of similar growth in their business when markets in Asia are opened to them. The Panamanian government is also contributing a share of the $50 million payment the United States made when it took over the construction of the canal from the French in 1902, when that nation's efforts to construct the canal failed. The business community in the country of Panama and the city of Colón includes a significant number of foreigners, some of them French businesspeople who chose to remain after their government canceled their role in constructing the canal, and others coming from various countries in Central and South America, where the canal's completion represented opportunity for financial gain. A large community of United States citizens has grown in the past several years, and represents a large portion of the managerial and technically skilled labor force that has been involved in construction of the canal and many of the ancillary development projects associated with it. The deepwater port of Colón is one of these projects.

The schedule is tight, in part because the canal continued to be a high-risk venture in its early years; the same dangers of mosquito-borne diseases, poor weather conditions, and the sheer technical challenge of the construction of a nearly 50-mile canal connecting the Atlantic and Pacific Oceans. When it became apparent that successful completion of the canal was likely under American management, the Panamanian government began looking for opportunities to capitalize on the largely American-owned asset that would make it a center of international commerce, and with the capital of Panama City already on the Pacific Coast, the commercial development of Colón and the relocation of sections of the railroad became a priority. The government deemed it a "nationally significant project," which qualified it for a no-bid, design-build contract that was awarded to the San Miguelito Construction Company, one of the Panamanian corporations with significant experience building the canal. With this "nationally significant project" status, San Miguelito Construction was also authorized to subcontract with other companies, including those owned by foreign nationals, as long as the total amount of work subcontracted to foreign companies did not exceed 49 percent of the total value of the contract.

As you will soon discover in your work as project manager for the three subunits that comprise the Colón deepwater port project, there are a number of strange business practices, unorthodox financial arrangements, and unusual individual team members associated with each of the three units you must control and manage in order to complete the work in time to meet the December 1913 deadline.

A Brief Introduction to Panama, Its Neighboring Countries, and the Global Superpowers of 1907

Without getting lost in details that can be their own distractions from the key lessons for today's project managers included in this historical fiction, let us set the stage a bit before we proceed. As we've described, you the reader have been selected as project manager for the Colón Deepwater Port Project. You have been hired by the San Miguelito Construction Company based in San Miguelito, Panama, which is 100 percent owned by the Lopez family, which came from Mexico in 1902 immediately following the Panamanian Revolution and the country's liberation from Colombia.

Your name is Samuel Anderson, and you are an American citizen recruited and hired by the Lopez family for what appears to be the opportunity of a lifetime. You are experienced in the work involved, having served as project manager for the development of new port facilities in Baltimore, Maryland; Savannah, Georgia; and Portland, Maine. Still, you hadn't applied for the job and only learned about it when you received an official letter from Fulgencio Lopez, president of San Miguelito Construction Company, in the summer of 1906. When you sailed to Colón to meet him, he informed you that you came highly recommended by Woodrow Farnsworth, a senior executive of the American company in charge of building the locks, seawalls, and other components of the canal's infrastructure. You had worked with Woodrow Farnsworth on the Baltimore project, and he was greatly impressed with your capabilities, as Fulgencio Lopez told you when the two of you met.

Fulgencio introduced you to several of his project team members, including the Panamanian nationals who served as his employees, and a French national, Pierre Rodista, who had worked on the canal when it was a French undertaking as a member of the engineering department. He remained on the site after the French team departed in 1902, and appeared to be a man of great influence. As Fulgencio Lopez said, Pierre Rodista had been granted Panamanian citizenship a few years later, a status that allowed him to form his own engineering company and be hired as a subcontractor to San Miguelito Construction without counting as a foreign national. What was odd about Pierre Rodista is that, despite your belief that he speaks fluent English, he only conversed with Fulgencio Lopez in Spanish, leaving it to him to translate Pierre's side of the conversation to you in English. But more about Pierre Rodista and Fulgencio Lopez later.

The international background of the Panama Canal project had its own intrigue. While Costa Rica, Nicaragua, and Mexico to the north represented little in the way of surprises or mystery, that was not the case with the four countries to the south and west of the canal. Colombia was understandably wary of the development of the canal, still smarting from the US-sponsored "revolution" that severed its province of Panama and made it a sovereign nation, immediately agreeing to lease terms for the canal zone that Colombia thought were skewed far too much in favor of the United States. Still, Colombia already has ports on the Atlantic and Pacific Oceans, so the addition of a canal wouldn't be as much of a boon to their economy as it would be to other countries with access to only one.

Peru, Bolivia, and Chile were three such countries, all of which had ports on the Pacific Ocean in the late nineteenth century. But they fought the "War of the Pacific" from 1879 through 1883, with Peru and Bolivia on one side and Chile on the other. Chile won, and claimed land from Bolivia that took away that country's only access to the sea, making it a landlocked nation. Even with the 1904 "Treaty of Peace and Friendship" between Chile and Bolivia, which granted Bolivia "unrestricted commercial transit through Chilean territory and ports in perpetuity," there was still bad blood between Chile and its northern neighbors. Bolivia had gone so far as to commission its own navy, although the only waters it could patrol were those of Lake Titicaca, on the border of Bolivia and Peru. While it is the largest lake in South America, it is landlocked, and the Bolivian Navy has always been more a stubborn statement of national pride than a real military force.

The canal under construction in the early 20th century.

Along with Ecuador, which did not share in the intrigue of its three neighbors, these four countries all had substantial interest in development of a port on the Atlantic side of the canal, since it would provide the opportunity to ship minerals and agricultural products through the canal to Colón, where these commodities could be transferred to Transatlantic freighters destined for Europe and Africa. European countries interested in the port of Colón included England, France, and Germany, which along with the United States, can be considered the global superpowers of the 1912, with the possible addition of Spain. Business people, diplomats, and skilled engineering professionals from all of these countries had come to Panama during the construction of the canal, some as early as the late decades of the nineteenth century, when the French were in charge.

The dominant currency in the world in 1907 was the British pound sterling, which was based on that nation's gold reserves, a standard that would end with the outbreak of World War I in 1914. The United States dollar was in the process of transitioning from a "hard" currency linked to the silver standard to the modern Federal Reserve System, which would be established in 1912. In reality, access to credit at the levels we expect in today's world was more limited at the time, so we will play our game with an international financial system more like the one in today's world than the one actually in place in Central America in 1907. In other words, while it might have been the norm for countries and corporations to pay for products and services with actual gold or silver or notes tied to specific national reserves of these precious metals, we will assume the availability of payment by paper checks without becoming distracted by the question of how things were done a century ago. This will be important for us later in this chapter as we discuss payment methods as a way to detect the possibility of a secret political or corrupt agenda in our projects.

With a final reminder that there are no airplanes in the skies and electronic business communications limited to those that can be transmitted by wire, we can resume telling the story—your story—of Samuel Anderson and his adventures as project manager of the Colón Deepwater Port project. In order to illustrate in more detail how the concepts introduced in earlier chapters of this book might appear in your project, we have separated them into three distinct "adventures."

Adventure #1: Why Is the Budget Twice What it Should Be?

Shortly after moving himself and his family into a well-appointed home in Colón and becoming familiar with his project headquarters office not far away, Samuel Anderson discovers that the budget he has been given is twice what it ought to be for the construction of the docks (the first third of the project), given the scope of work. Payments are flowing from the Panamanian Central Bank (part of the country's government) to San Miguelito Construction Company in these higher amounts, and everyone seems to be happy. Pierre Rodista, who is serving as project engineer and quantity surveyor, approves these payments and routinely reports to Samuel that all is going well. Similarly, the president of Panama, Manuel Amador Guerrero, is satisfied with the project, which Samuel can still manage without being affected by the cost overruns. They bother Samuel, and he wants to know what is happening, since he feels responsible for delivering a project within his own standards of cost effectiveness.

He discovers that money is actually being funneled from European investors—principally the French—to pay for the development of a secret naval base on the Atlantic Coast of Costa Rica. This base, complete with port facilities and even warships, is being funded by money flowing from France to Panama to San Miguelito Construction Company, which in turn pays more than the market price for work performed by subcontractors from Peru and Chile. These subcontractors in turn send the money to other companies in their countries for construction of warships, and to Costa Rica for construction of the naval port. The purpose of this naval facility is to protect Colón from possible naval bombardment or a seaborne invasion of the canal by possible hostile powers, like England, or the United States, or Spain. Pierre Rodista is a major reason why this secret project scope is in place, and Samuel is powerless to stop him.

Still, there is no immediate reason for Samuel to do so, since no one else seems to care; even individuals and corporations and government officials he believes know exactly what is going on. As an official citizen of Panama, Pierre Rodista is capable of free movement in and around the country, and the trust of the Panamanian government—in a way other foreign national are not—including Samuel Anderson.

Thus, Samuel is faced with his first choice based on the realization that his project—as valuable as it will be to the nation of Panama and international commerce—is larger, more complex, and frankly, more political in nature than he had previously known or even imagined. He is nominally responsible for a budget that is double what he believes is required to complete the docks in Colón's new deepwater port, although in a sense he is still "succeeding" in the eyes of the bankers, government officials, and even the president of Panama. Officials at the San Miguelito Construction Company are only too happy to invoice the Panamanian Central Bank for the larger-than-necessary payments, and to ask Samuel to assist in both submitting these invoices and distributing the expected payments to various subcontractors, including the ones who are clearly being paid far more than they "should" be, based on Samuel's professional expertise. Pierre Rodista is always present when these extraordinary payments are either being received or paid, along with several shadowy associates he brings with him, depending on the subcontractor involved in each particular transaction.

Surprisingly, even though Samuel believes the payments he is directing to certain subcontractors are questionable and might be illegal, they are drawn as official bank drafts, and are not being made in cash, as he might expect them to be. If the Panamanian Central Bank is willing to stand behind these payments, there is little chance that "exposing" secret payments would be something Samuel could do. He is simply building a very expensive system of docks at a new port that is strategically vital to the country where he is working. And while there are a number of individuals and companies that seem to be taking certain payments for use in projects that are not part of the docks Samuel is responsible for constructing, there are other companies that are doing precisely what they are supposed to do. The docks can be built, on a schedule that will allow them to be completed by the December 1913 deadline: the engineering specifications are consistent with the port's intended use for international shipping, and construction methods and materials also meet Samuel's quality standards.

Any doubts about the likely outcome if Samuel Anderson were to register a formal complaint about the payments being shepherded through his project via Pierre Rodista and his colleagues were removed in the first project review meeting with Samuel's boss, Fulgencio Lopez of San Miguelito Construction Company, the mayor of Colón, representatives of the Panamanian Central Bank, the president of Panama himself, Pierre Rodista (of course), and a larger team of representatives of the Panamanian armed forces—a surprising group of admirals and generals Samuel had never met before. The meeting, held at an elaborate dinner at the mayor's private residence, was largely a celebration of the project. President Guerrero personally thanked everyone, including Samuel Anderson, for their "great service on behalf of the Panamanian people," in a short English-language address. Afterwards, over brandy and cigars, many of the individuals attending the dinner—essentially a "who's who" of powerful financial and political leaders in the nation of Panama—personally greeted Samuel, offering their assistance in helping him achieve the port project's objectives.

Samuel Anderson knew he had no rational hope of "blowing the whistle" on Pierre Rodista's questionable activities, or the fact that payments were clearly being routed to projects beyond his management or knowledge. On the other hand, he also knew that the Colón Deepwater Port Project was an important endeavor for the city and for the country of Panama, and that he would have the financial resources and official government support needed to successfully complete it. Further, he had confidence in his team of local engineers, contractors, and fellow managers at San Miguelito Construction Company—and how his own skills and experience could help the project succeed. Still, he had to make the difficult choice of remaining on the project despite the presence of Pierre Rodista and his knowledge that much of the money included in his project budget was being diverted to the construction of a secret naval base in Costa Rica, or resigning and returning with his family to the United States. Given all of these considerations, what did Samuel do?

He stayed.

Adventure #2: Who Are These People?

A little more than a year later, in the spring of 1908, Samuel Anderson received a letter from President Guerrero, introducing two young men from Mexico who would be coming to Samuel's office to meet with him on Wednesday, April 8. The president asked Samuel to ensure that he and his staff would show the young men every courtesy and to give their business proposal "serious consideration." However, other than their names—Antonio Santos and Tomaso Santiago—and the fact that they were "young men," the president's letter said nothing about the matter the two young men wanted to discuss.

When he arrived at his office on Wednesday, April 8, Samuel found young Antonio and Tomaso with his secretary Anita Jones waiting for their meeting. They were sipping coffee Anita had provided while waiting for him, and after exchanging pleasantries, he excused himself for a moment for a private review of his day's agenda with Anita in his office. Once he and Anita had confirmed plans for the day—a routine review of construction progress on the docks with his foreman and a presentation on the financial status of the adjacent ship maintenance facility—he asked her to escort his guests into his office for their meeting.

Once they settled in and Anita closed the door, their meeting began. Antonio and Tomaso did not speak English well, so they conducted their meeting in Spanish; Samuel was fluent in the language, so there was no need for an interpreter. The two young men quickly informed Samuel that they represented Majestuoso Construction Company, a Panamanian corporation they co-owned, and that they had been invited to be part of the third of three projects Samuel Anderson was overseeing—relocation of the transcontinental Panamanian Railroad. They informed Samuel that although they were born in Mexico, they had been granted Panamanian citizenship by President Guerrero, and that he suggested they meet with Samuel as the first order of business in their new role as members of the project's ship maintenance facilities and drydock.

Samuel Anderson thought this was a bit strange, since the ship maintenance facility team was already in place; he had hired many of them himself, including subcontractors. Still, Antonio and Tomaso expressed their keen interest in working closely with Samuel Anderson as members of his port maintenance facility team, letting him know that they believed the two of them could make his work "mucho mas facíl" (much easier). Even more surprising, as the meeting progressed and Samuel began discussing the details of the project, it became clear that the two young men had little if any experience in the construction business. Their company was new, as they explained, and this was their first major assignment. They said that President Guerrero had told them to contact Samuel first because he could teach them the skills they would need to carry out their assignment, and because, as they also told him, they were very quick learners.

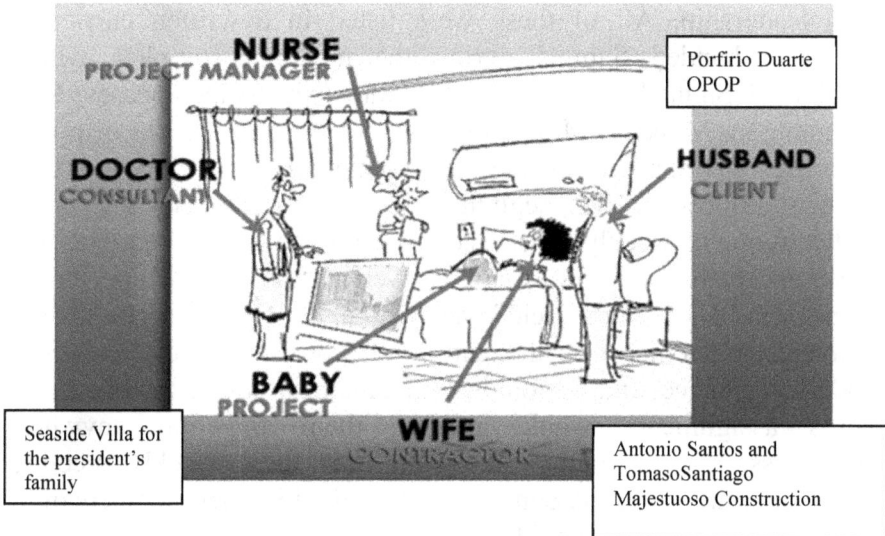

Remembering the president's request to show them every courtesy, Samuel welcomed them as members of his team and promised that he would do all he could to orient them to the project. As the meeting concluded, Antonio and Tomaso told him that they were in the process of setting up the home office for Majestuoso Construction Company nearby in Colón, and looked forward to their next meeting. Then they excused themselves and left, thanking Samuel politely if a bit profusely for his time. Samuel knew better than to call President Guerrero to ask him what in the world was going on, and instead sent a letter by special delivery to Fulgencio Lopez, his boss, to ask if he could provide any additional information about the two young men. Fulgencio suggested that they discuss the matter during their next regular weekly meeting the following Friday.

Among the many other agenda items that day, Samuel was even more surprised to learn that Fulgencio Lopez and his senior management team had decided on a formal training program for the two young men from Mexico, and that Samuel Anderson was in charge of it. They needed to learn a broad range of skills, from procurement to liaison with the construction company's engineering department to financial management, personnel management, and team leadership. All of these were listed in a written curriculum Fulgencio handed Samuel during the meeting, complete with a division of Samuel's teaching duties into two distinct phases. First, beginning on Monday, May 4, there would be three months of private "tutoring" by Samuel for the two young men in these and other subjects. Following that, beginning in August, Samuel's role would switch to one of weekly supervision meetings in Colón regarding their work, except for such times as they were in the field. The reference about them being "in the field" was particularly strange, since the port maintenance facility was the part of the project closest to Samuel Anderson's office, and he couldn't imagine how any of the two young men's assignments would require them traveling anywhere. Regardless, the curriculum described how these weekly meetings would be similar to those Samuel conducted with other members of his team, except that they would continue to include educational services "based on the judgment of the project manager (Samuel Anderson) that such education is necessary for the continued success of Majestuoso Construction Company in its work."

Samuel had never seen anything like it, even though he had become accustomed to the fact that certain aspects of the project might evolve via unpredictable, even sudden changes. He agreed to Fulgencio's directive that he take the two young men under his wing, and set out to prepare the details of the curriculum that was only outlined in the five-page curriculum he was given by Fulgencio Lopez. And on the first Monday of May, he began his project management education program for his two young protégés, as requested. Samuel was a good teacher, having actually been on the faculty of the Massachusetts College of Art and Design in the late 1870s, and later at the Boston Architectural Club (now the Boston Architectural College) when it was founded in 1889. In his opinion, Antonio Santos and Tomaso Santiago were "average" students, confident in their abilities but not particularly dedicated to the details of the disciplines they would need to know in order to successfully manage a project of the size and scale of Colón's new port maintenance facility. But to Samuel's amazement, as the first three months of their studies proceeded, Antonio and Tomaso attended every important meeting of the entire project team, including not only the maintenance facility, but also the dockyards and even the team working on the relocation of Panama's transcontinental railway. They were treated as equals by other members of the team; some of the subcontractors were even deferential to them. It was obvious that these inexperienced young men were powerful in a way that was beyond Samuel's ability to understand, and no one had a good answer why except to say that they had the "full confidence of President Guerrero."

When the three-month tutoring program concluded, Antonio and Tomaso began working with the staff of San Miguelito Construction Company on the port maintenance facility, working under the company's managers responsible for that aspect of the overall project. These managers' reports of their work were always glowing if general in nature. It was apparent that everyone was happy with their work, although Samuel was unable to get anything but the most general evaluations of their contributions. Samuel was concerned that he had another mysterious parallel project on his hands, although, as he had learned, their arrival didn't necessarily cause the overall project to lag in terms of its schedule, budget, or quality performance. The additional funds to be paid to Majestuoso Construction Company were somehow already included in the overall budget for the port maintenance facility, and were forecast to begin in May of 1908 as "additional subcontractor, port maintenance." Since this was precisely the month in which they arrived on the scene, it was apparent to Samuel that, even though it was a surprise to him, it was right on schedule for whoever was overseeing the project budget.

This all changed one day in the fall of 1908 when the two young men suddenly disappeared, and could not be found for several weeks. Since Samuel felt responsible for their well-being as their teacher and mentor, he made a number of inquiries about them, believing he if anyone should have answers for President Guerrero if he should ask what had happened to them. Through Samuel's network of friends in high places within the Panamanian government, he soon learned that they were in trouble with none other than the president himself. In learning this startling fact, he also learned the true nature of Majestuoso Construction Company's primary and secret mission in the overall project. They were actually charged with siphoning project funds away from the construction of the ship maintenance and construction facility and directing these funds toward the building of a seaside villa for the president's family on the Pacific Coast of Panama, more than fifty miles away. This villa, far enough away from Colón for Samuel Anderson to have any idea of its existence, was well underway in its construction; its existence went a long way to explaining why Antonio and Tomaso would sometimes notify Samuel that they would be "in the field" for a week or two at various times when their work should have been no more than a few blocks away.

What even Fulgencio Lopez and his senior managers at San Miguelito Construction Company didn't know is that Antonio and Tomaso had been stealing some of the money they were supposed to be diverting to the construction of President Guerrero's villa for themselves along the way. It became apparent when a few government official witnessed them "living beyond their means" during their frequent visits to Panama City while they were officially supervising construction of the villa a few miles to the west. Samuel was never able to learn what "living beyond their means" really meant, but it didn't matter. He was glad to know that whatever had happened to his young team members was official government business, even if their sudden disappearance was unnerving. After several weeks they returned to Colón with a bit less swagger and arrogance, but amazingly they simply resumed their work and the government continued to praise it as "excellent," which Samuel had come to understand meant that construction of the villa on the coast was proceeding quite nicely.

Thinking back on the details of how the two young men and their equally new company came upon the scene in the spring, Samuel recalled a few aspects of their business arrangements that were also unusual. First, even though the master project budget controlled by San Miguelito Construction Company included a line item covering their arrival on the job, they received an extraordinary initial payment of 40 percent of their total contract amount, much higher than the 10 percent to 15 percent Samuel was used to seeing in the project to date. Even more unusual, payment was in gold bullion from the Panamanian National Bank, delivered to the new company shortly after their arrival in May. That should have been alarming in and of itself, although Samuel was distracted by the need to develop an educational curriculum, and had learned that there might be occasional odd aspects of the overall project. As long as these unusual events didn't affect the progress of the docks, the shipyard, or the railroad—and the mysterious scope of work given to Antonio and Tomaso did not do any of these things—he could be curious about these parallel agendas but could continue to dedicate himself to carrying out his official duties. And other than a sense of alarm for the young men's well-being while they were missing, their absence caused no disruption in the progress of the ship maintenance facility project. Truth be told, the schedule was never really affected when they were present, either. Still, even though everything returned to "normal" once the two men returned, and Samuel was able to learn the real reason for their presence in the project, Samuel is left to contemplate the overall meaning of this second adventure.

He concludes that there are three major lessons. First, by paying close attention to details like the sudden appearance of unqualified team members or the payment of unusual fees in gold bullion, he might be able to better understand the overall project and predict which parts of it might be corrupt and deserving of more cautious management. These aspects of the project might be dangerous and unpredictable, but they can also be far enough removed from the "real" project details for which Samuel is responsible that he can largely ignore them and concentrate on his official duties. Second, he was almost reassured that there was a kind of authority monitoring the entire project, and that individuals like young Antonio and Tomaso were not beyond being apprehended and punished for being personally corrupt. And third—related to the second lesson—Samuel could take some comfort in the belief that if he maintained his own high ethical standards in his work, he could succeed in completing the docks, shipyards, and railway despite the other aspects of the project that were out of his control. There were risks he would rather not be part of his work, of course, but he had learned that his dedication to his professional responsibilities and his honest application of his skills and best judgment had won him the confidence of his colleagues, even as some of these colleagues were tolerating or directing activities that were alarming to Samuel. But as long as Samuel was consistently working toward the successful completion of work under his control, he was becoming increasingly confident that he would be not only allowed to continue his work, but would leave Colón and Panama all the better for his time working there.

Adventure #3: Why Can't I Find This Company in the Panamanian Registry of Corporations?

The third of Samuel Anderson's three-project units—the relocation of the Panamanian transcontinental railroad—was probably always going to be the most difficult one to manage. First of all, even though "transcontinental" really means fewer than fifty miles from the Atlantic to the Pacific in Panama, it still required significant remote management from Samuel's headquarters office in Colón. And second, as he would learn, rerouting the railway involved the consideration of many more factors than the intrusion of the canal on the right-of-way of the original railroad when it was constructed a half-century earlier. The precise routing of the railway's new sections was the subject of complex negotiations, with several landowners and representatives of Panamanian corporations and the military requesting that the railway either be located near their properties in some cases, or as far away as possible in others. Finally, the Panamanian organization responsible for approving the rerouting of the railway and for engineering its new construction presented the most serious and dangerous aspect of the project of all. This was the Panamanian Oficina de Proyectos de Obra Pública (OPOP), or the Panamanian Office of Public Engineering Projects, headed by Porfirio Duarte, a mysterious, powerful, and fearsome figure.

Panamanians in 1907 still had compelling (and true) historical memories of the power a railroad can have on the development—or conversely the ruin—of a local economy. In 1855, when the railway was completed, it was still fourteen years before the completion of the United States Transcontinental Railroad in 1869. For these fourteen years, the Panamanian railway was the first and only transcontinental rail link between the Atlantic and the Pacific, and it brought millions of dollars in revenue to Colombia (at the time, Panama was a province of this nation). During its heyday, the Panamanian transcontinental railway transported freight, passengers, and gold bullion safely from coast to coast, greatly increasing international and even US interstate trade between ships dropping off and picking up cargo and passengers at Panama's Atlantic and Pacific port cities. Conversely, when its Atlantic terminus in Colón started operating, the railway essentially destroyed the previous Atlantic port city of Chagres, which was soon abandoned in favor of the new port and today is no more than a tiny village. And finally, after the United States transcontinental railroad was completed in 1869, the Panamanian transcontinental railroad's value fell sharply, and it became essentially bankrupt ten years later.[1]

Rerouting the railroad to make way for the canal was a big deal for Panamanians in 1907, even though in more recent years the railway was no longer as lucrative as it had been in the decade and a half after it opened. Still it was considered a strategic necessity, in case the canal were to be shut down for any reason (landslide, mechanical failure of its lock system, or hostile military actions), or as a way to conduct official monitoring and maintenance activities of the canal. While engineering studies had begun a year earlier, the final route of the railway was still uncertain in 1907. Property owners or businesses that could benefit from location of the railway nearby—tourist locations, manufacturing facilities, and military installations, for example—were still lobbying for such relocation, while others who opposed the presence of noisy, smoke-belching locomotives or rails and ties bisecting their land—owners of vacation villas and large plantations—lobbied equally hard to move the new rail right-of-way as far away as possible.

The organization officially charged with approving the final route of the railway, the OPOP, therefore had great power to make or break the financial health of property owners who might be affected by the final location of the new transcontinental railway. And its shadowy chief, Porfirio Duarte, wielded this power ruthlessly, secretly, and without recourse. Samuel Anderson first learned about him when he called his first team meeting for the railway unit of his overall project and learned firsthand about his colleague's concern and even fear of Porfirio Duarte. They were unwilling to begin any construction activities until they believed they had the assurance of Duarte's and the OPOP's approval. But when Samuel would ask them how to communicate with this mysterious agency and its powerful chief, he was met with silence. They suggested going through President Guerrero, although after the meeting, one of his colleagues at San Miguelito Construction Company told Samuel that even the president might be powerless to stop Mr. Duarte from doing whatever he wanted, with little or no prior notice. Even more serious, when Samuel asked what "doing whatever he wanted" meant, he was told that there was no limit on these possibilities, including financial sanctions against companies or individuals on whom Duarte wanted to take revenge, or even imprisonment or physical violence against individuals, even those considered to be powerful and beyond the reach of extralegal persecution.

These discussions in the summer of 1907 gave Samuel Anderson pause. He needed to begin construction of the railroad in order to meet his December 1913 deadline, and he had a number of engineering studies and "preliminary" route approvals in hand from work begun in 1906, before his arrival on the project. Could he move forward with the plans conducted by San Miguelito Construction Company's engineers, or did he need to ensure final approval by the Panamanian government and this mysterious OPOP and Porfirio Duarte? His instincts told him that—given his methodical approach to date and the fact that his careful attention to professionalism, ethical behavior, and confidentiality in the face of activities he found troublesome—he could win approval of a route with relatively few difficulties, but he wanted to do his homework before deciding his next step. So he ventured to Panama City (via the railway, which was still operational despite canal construction) to meet with the country's economic ministers and learn what he could about OPOP and its powerful chief.

When he arrived, he found a similar reluctance to discuss either the agency or the man. He was told that OPOP was an independent organization and not an official branch of the Panamanian government. This was surprising news, but at least it gave him someplace to go to learn more about it. He decided to consult the country's official registry of corporations at the Ministry of the Economy, and made arrangements for an official visit through his contacts at the Office of the President. He arrived at the Ministry's Hall of Records the morning after receiving permission, searching the directory of corporations for references to OPOP as his first order of business. He found no reference for it in any of the documents or files he would expect to contain this information. When he inquired about this apparent oversight, ministry officials told him that they would need to check with their superiors and get back to him. Samuel then tried a secondary plan, which was to look for any information in the directory of business managers, a separate document and library. There, he hit a similar brick wall. There was no reference anywhere for Porfirio Duarte, even though he believed someone this powerful would have to be recognized for past accomplishments or even educational credentials to justify his position. Again he asked ministry officials about the matter, and they gave him a similar answer. They would check with their superiors and get back to him.

Samuel returned to Colón with no information about OPOP or Porfirio Duarte, and with no reliable guidance on how to proceed— except for his own realization that it was time to begin construction in order to meet his deadline, and a second realization that he was navigating dangerous political waters. He decided that the only person who would know how to manage around this roadblock wasn't a political leader but would in fact be a businessman, ideally in the construction industry. He would trust Fulgencio Lopez, his boss, to help him find the right person—one who could tell him how the OPOP operates in real life, and how to avoid the very real dangers of running afoul of its leader, Porfirio Duarte. They met for dinner shortly after

Samuel's return, and Fulgencio suggested his father, Rodrigo Lopez, who had founded San Miguelito Construction Company in 1882 and retired more than ten years ago. Fulgencio said he had promised his father to never bring him back into the business so he could enjoy his retirement, but he believed this was a special challenge that warranted consulting the old man, something he had done only once before, during the turbulent year when the Americans bought the canal project from the French, and the Panamanian Revolution created an independent nation. Rodrigo had helped his son then, and he was the only person who could reliably help Samuel now.

Samuel was amazed to find that what should have been a routine—if politically charged—process for receiving final approval of a railway right-of-way would in fact be on par with something as important as the origins of the American canal project, including a political revolution and the birth of a new nation. His sense of the danger he faced wasn't diminished, but at least he believed he was going to get the best guidance on how to proceed that he could find. Fulgencio told him that they would need to go to his father's plantation near Gatun, which had become a sleepy seaside resort, far different from its days as a busy seaport on the Atlantic coast. It would require automobile transportation over mostly dirt roads, but Fulgencio assured him that his father's villa was comfortable and would be a fine location for their important discussion. They left a few days later for a twenty-mile trip. It took nearly an entire day.

"Welcome, my son," Rodrigo said as they arrive. "And welcome to you as well, Señor Anderson. My son has told me all about you." Samuel was impressed with the old man's presence. He was well over the age of eighty, but he was physically strong and his mind was sharp. Samuel and Fulgencio took a short time to wash up and dress for dinner; they would stay the night and continue their talks into the following day.

At dinner, Rodrigo Lopez regaled them with stories of the old days in the Panamanian construction business, before the advent of automobiles, when railways were the primary way of moving construction equipment, and how many of these rail lines were designed to be temporary in nature, requiring accelerated construction schedules based on the short lifespans of these railways. They talked about how the French had begun work on their canal with much promise, but got into various troubles and lost their way. He had great confidence in the Americans and told Samuel that he sincerely believed that his professional skills and expertise would help ensure the successful completion of the port and railway. Samuel, knowing the importance of personal relationships in Panama, returned the old man's good wishes with compliments about his achievements, which he had made a point of researching in advance of their visit.

The conversation eventually moved to OPOP and Porfirio Duarte, and how important and truly independent the man and his organization had become. Manuel Amador Guerrero was the first president of Panama, and had been in power only since 1904. Therefore, while he was generally respected and trusted by the Panamanian people, he still maneuvered in a political world that included rival centers of power and strongmen who were unwilling to give up their fiefdoms to the new president or his government. One of these men was Porfirio Duarte, who commanded significant loyalty from several Panamanian businessmen and political leaders and wasn't shy about using this loyalty as the basis for creating an independent power base in the new country. While President Guerrero's background was as a physician and railroad management—he was the official doctor of the Panamanian Railway—he was not a businessman in the same way Porfirio Duarte and some of his colleagues were. Manuel Amador Guerrero was a great revolutionary leader but he was a careful president, and he didn't challenge his fellow Panamanian leaders in the same way he stood up to Colombia when fighting for his nation's independence in 1903. He would allow Porfirio Duarte great leeway in whatever role Duarte had carved out for himself, which was essentially presiding over important economic developments in the country. Duarte had a background in engineering, and he used this technical expertise to position OPOP as a reviewer of economic projects in Panama. While the agency was independent of the government, he made its official mission one of formal review before important projects could proceed. Duarte used his background in engineering to maintain public credibility for his power of review, although in practice he wielded power based on many factors beyond the engineering quality of new projects alone. And President Guerrero tolerated his activities, because he didn't want to risk a power struggle with Duarte at such a sensitive time in the development of his new nation.

Rodrigo continued their dinner conversation as he shifted from storytelling alone to the delivery of sound advice on how to proceed with the railway. "I want nothing more than the success of the new railroad, and you can be sure that President Guerrero feels the same way, especially given his years of service to the original transcontinental railway," Rodrigo Lopez told his son and Samuel. "If you need the president's intervention, he will eventually act on your behalf, but it is best if you proceed without needing him. And I believe that Porfirio Duarte will allow you to construct the railroad as long as you give him the time he needs to make the key decisions about where it will be located. The secret is that he wants to be able to reward some of his old colleagues for their work on behalf of the revolution and perhaps their personal service to him in his business ventures. If you approach him with a request for final routing of the railway's new sections and allow him to manage the process of consulting with the landowners in question, I believe you'll find him to be most reasonable. The problems with old Porfirio will only come if he feels he is being disrespected. And President Guerrero will tell you that, as a doctor, he personally treated the injuries of more than a few important individuals in Panama who thought they could ignore old Porfirio in their decision-making. Pay him respect and he will honor your interests. But try to circumvent him and OPOP at your peril."

Rodrigo then turned to Samuel Anderson and told him, "Remember, my friend, you wouldn't be here in your job today if Porfirio Duarte hadn't approved of the idea. He therefore believes you owe him the courtesy of allowing him to participate in the decisions on where to locate the railway. He won't necessarily want to meet with you to discuss the route, he's not interested in abstract discussions. My son can help you get the message to him that you want his help in this matter, and he will gladly give it to you." With that final bit of advice, the old man suggested they retire for the evening, but not before sharing the finest Cuban rum and cigars.

The next day, as they drove back to Colón, Fulgencio Lopez assured Samuel that he would arrange for a communication with Porfirio Duarte and OPOP. But it would require Samuel to agree that this communication would be managed by Fulgencio, and that Samuel would further agree to making changes to Porfirio's decision only based on technical or engineering concerns, and not for any other reasons. Fulgencio told Samuel he would bring a minimum of these objections from Samuel back to OPOP for final review, and that while he couldn't guarantee what Porfirio Duarte's final decision might be, this process would end with formal approval by OPOP. And this final approval would allow the railway project relocation to move forward. After that approval, Samuel could be assured that he could manage this third unit of the project's budget, schedule, and quality performance to the same extent he had already been managing the dockyards and ship maintenance facility.

It was not a complete victory for Samuel Anderson but, in his opinion, it was a victory for the overall project. He agreed to the process Fulgencio Lopez had proposed, and thanked his boss for his help, particularly in arranging for the meeting with his father. Samuel had successfully navigated the dangerous political waters of project management in Panama in the early years of this new nation and work that the country's leaders wanted to be done as the American efforts to build the Panama Canal continued. He had done so in three separate adventures, each more difficult than the previous one. And in the process, he had maintained his professional and ethical standards as much as humanly possible. There was no government agency charged with the maintenance of professional behavior on a construction project in Panama, and he was hired because of his experience and reputation alone, not through any formal licensing or accreditation process. If he had not been able to call on his own personal reservoirs of skill and experience, or if he didn't have access to the help of individuals like Fulgencio and Rodrigo Lopez, he might have failed. But he didn't fail, even if he had to face great personal risk at times in his work. In the next two chapters, we will explore how the fictional experience of Samuel Anderson compares and contrasts with the experiences of modern-day project managers in the United States, and what we can do to enhance and ensure their ability to rely on their professionalism without resorting to the kinds of help Samuel Anderson was forced to find in Panama in 1907.

Chapter 5

Cities, Not Walls—A Design Solution for Today's World

Border Cities: A Design Solution that Connects—Not Divides— People and Societies

"In an age where the world is increasingly connected and homogeneous, to seek regional presence and that otherness in architecture hinges on a relevant, reconnection of values: between those of the past and the present, and those local and universal. Herein lies the essence of sustainability and authenticity in architecture."[2]

~ *Peter Cook,* Reconnecting Cultures: The Architecture of Rocco Design

The link between architecture and values—those of individuals, cultures, and political societies—cannot be ignored. That link can be seen in sharp focus in the politics of the United States in 2017, more than a hundred years later than the world we have just visited with Samuel Anderson. Still, there are ideas held by current political leaders that are as out of date as the Panamanian government's belief that a railway near the Panama Canal might have value for any reason beyond its use to transport goods and passengers during an emergency shutdown of the canal, or as a way of transporting maintenance personnel and equipment without disrupting the use of the canal for its intended purpose of promoting international trade. One of these obsolete ideas is the belief that a border wall between this country and Mexico can bring security and safety to American citizens. Building it is a priority for President Donald Trump's administration, demonstrating a novel way in which a political agenda can intrude in a way that detracts from a more carefully considered method for promoting security, increasing new economic opportunities (i.e. jobs), and creating connections among people, which are three important contributions a well-designed construction or development project can make to the society where it is located.

Ironically, this political idea that separates people is coming to life at a time when the world has never been more interconnected. Transportation, trade, communications media, and international cooperation have never been more efficient at linking any one individual with any other, in anyplace across the world. The same can be said for the interconnection of countries, of cultures, and of economic enterprises. The idea of a wall that separates people from each other can be seen as an anachronism, an idea whose time has passed long ago, and an idea that will never work.

As stated in the above quote, the essence of sustainability and authenticity in architecture hinges on connections, not division. Peter Cook notes that these connections are not only among people, cultures, and social structures in the present; they also connect with values that transcend the boundaries of geography and time. Respect for these values is what defines architectural design in terms of its quality and sustainability. It is ironic that anyone would believe the use of architecture that prevents free and open access of people, ideas, and values can do anything to keep people secure in today's world. And yet this is exactly what the US Department of Homeland Security has sought in its request for proposals for a border wall earlier this year.

A radical yet practical idea: border cities

Our idea is to replace walls with a development that attracts people from both sides of any border—not just the one between the United States and Mexico—and with them the ideas, commerce, values, and sustainability that go with these connections. Border cities will make the nations on either side more secure, not less, and can also eliminate the need for people of either nation to leave their homes to realize the benefits of this new development. Border cities will foster and expand the interconnectivity among people and cultures, and, as we will see in the writings of other designers, will make both countries more secure, not less.

What is a Border City? And how will it work? Questions to consider.

There are a number of practical questions raised by people when the idea of a border city is introduced. The most basic one is, "Why build these cities at all?" Why will people from Mexico want to go to these cities? Will they go there to seek healthcare, jobs, or an education? What is preventing them from getting these same services and benefits in their home country? Is it the lack of resources? Is it a lack of political will to create these services and benefits on the part of the Mexican government? Access to healthcare, jobs, and education has long been a reason for people to emigrate to the United States; why does seeking these amenities require leaving one's home country? Can border cities answer this demand?

Similarly, what is preventing people from the United States investing in the creation of these services in Mexico today? Our belief is that because Mexico is another country, American citizens have no interest in making that type of investment, especially small businesses. There are different laws regarding property ownership and taxation, a new set of government regulations, different laws and law enforcement, and perhaps a lack of market demand and the financial means to justify a return on investment in a foreign country. But what if the idea of border cities becomes a reality and these new communities provide opportunities to rationalize the differences that prevent long-distance investment and compliance with new laws and regulations? What if the idea of connectivity is a basic concept for these cities, so that it is easy for citizens of both countries to invest there, find jobs there, enroll in school there, and get their healthcare there? What if border cities were designed to be "local" for each country?

Services in the Border Cities: Healthcare and Education

When it comes to services like healthcare, another obvious question is who will pay for these benefits? Who will build the clinics? What will be different about these cities to make care accessible for Mexican people who cannot get these services at home? If Mexican citizens cannot afford to travel to the United States to take advantage of these opportunities, how do they find the healthcare they need? When we think of countries with borders, we automatically think of the reasons why this access is difficult or even impossible. Money, skilled doctors, modern healthcare technology, healthcare network design including hospitals, community health centers, ambulances, and preventive health education programs can be seen as barriers that deny access to needed care. So can the lack of coordinated teams of healthcare professionals including doctors, surgeons and other specialists, nurses, medical technicians, health educators, health administrators, and even billing offices and insurance companies. These systems exist in much of the United States, but may not be as prevalent in Mexico. They are not trivial issues to solve, but in order to provide greater access to care, is building a wall the answer? Our argument is no; it is better to take the first step of designing border cities where there is at least the commitment to connect people with each other, and with the resources they need—like healthcare. Those values, and the belief that connectivity is a key first step in extending values across the boundaries of geography and time, are the hallmark of good architectural design.

The issue of education is similar to that of healthcare; it is a social benefit that people will seek when they move to these new border cities. How will the schools in these cities be different from other schools in Mexico? Why will they be different? Will they be based on the US system? What is currently preventing someone from opening a school in Mexico that is based on the US educational system? Again, the answers to these questions are not easy, and they will take time to develop—the same as other legitimate design questions. But the answers will never come if there is no commitment to find them. Whatever the reasons why there are no (or at least not enough) schools in Mexico based on the US system, the fact is that they are not currently being built on a large scale. Border cities are a design concept based on the idea that these types of schools can and should be built in a way that connects people. Walls only compound the current inequities and differences in opportunities; they do nothing to solve these issues. And, as I will argue later, walls in fact make these issues worse and harder to solve.

Employers and Employees: Who Will Work, and How Will They Be Hired?

And what about jobs? What type of jobs do people from both countries need? The majority of current employment opportunities for new immigrants in the United States involve the performance of physical labor—at other people's farms and construction sites, or in domestic service at their homes, for example. These jobs are rooted in the geography of where those farms, construction sites, and homes are located. They cannot be brought from the United States to Mexico. But border cities can be designed with employment opportunities as part of their very purpose. Manufacturing centers, retail outlet, and human services (including education and healthcare) can be designed as part of these new cities, so there will be jobs as well as services for people who will seek opportunities in these new urban areas. And if necessary, border cities can be located near agricultural lands to expand available employment and to provide food and other crops to support these new cities' economies.

Here again there are many practical questions to ask, and they deserve serious, well-conceived answers. But that is the point: instead of pointing out the reasons why new employment opportunities cannot be made available across the border between the United States and Mexico, why not start with the premise that a border city can be the spark that allows for collaboration on finding reasons why they can be created? Any of us can think of many reasons why the border city concept will never work. If the jobs in these cities are all based on cheap labor, then how will US citizens find work there? If everyone is paid the same, why will employers pay higher wages for unskilled labor? Why would employers pay higher wages at a border city factory than they would pay by locating a new facility in Mexico, away from the border?

These are real issues to solve, but our contention is that there is no such thing as a problem: there are only issues to solve. Statements such as "We can never set labor rates that will work for citizens of both the United States and Mexico in these cities" need to be replaced with "Why not?" questions, such as, "Why not find a way to set labor rates that work for citizens of both countries?" When we ask what types of jobs can be created and how the different expectations of employees from the United States and Mexico can be integrated, we are asking the kind of questions that create and support the connectivity that defines good design.

The Legal System: Which Country's Laws Will Prevail?

Another question relates to the legal system that will govern these border cities. Who has jurisdiction? If someone commits a crime, by what laws will that individual be judged? Will the laws be those of Mexico or the United States? If the laws in border cities are not going to be those of Mexico or the United States, who will create the new laws? How can border cities' legal systems be structured in a way that does not inadvertently create new borders separating them from both countries? In other words, how can border cities be designed so they do not become islands unto themselves? How can this very basic social structure be developed so it promotes interconnectivity and does not prevent it?

When it comes to questions like the one about border cities' legal systems, we have the opportunity to ask a countering question about the walls some seek to build. What is the legal structure that prevents, or at least limits, people from coming to the United States through legal means? Who benefits from these laws? Who are hurt? Are these laws necessary, or even just? Could the funds used to create and enforce these laws be used for a better purpose, such as the thorough design of border cities that seek to address these issues?

*Walls can divide cities. It is our argument that cities
can make walls obsolete.*

Summary: The Will to Solve These Issues Is a Vital First Step

There are two sides for each of the issues raised in this section. There are those who will want to live in border cities seeking to offer, give, or sell goods and services. There are also those who will seek to take, use, or buy. The same person can be on both sides of these exchanges in different situations. It is easy to imagine the incentive for people who seek to take, use, or buy health care, education, and jobs. The challenge is to identify and to fulfill the incentives for those who will offer, give, or sell these goods and services. Where can we begin the design challenge that seeks answers to these questions? Why do we believe border cities are uniquely capable of solving the issues found along the border between two countries? Why do we believe they offer a better answer than building a traditional wall?

The answer might be found in a closer look in two places: the history of city design and six design concepts that, when taken into consideration, can lead our search for the answers to the questions raised in this section:[3]

1. Identity: a resolution of a building's (or a city's) contents and use.
2. Spatiality: our perception of space, informed by the history of how people use and appreciate these spaces.
3. Community: a spirit of togetherness reflected in design.
4. Density: the balance between environmental sensitivity and human vitality.
5. Connectivity: the successful collision of people, objects, and information.
6. Materiality: understanding the properties of materials and selecting them for utility, form, and ability to evoke an emotional response.

A high-level look at the history of borders and cities can also shed some light on the practical questions that must be addressed in the design and development of border cities, and how the interconnectivity and values they represent can make borders vital places for community and economic activity while enhancing, not risking, security. It's surprising how relevant some of the thinking about these subjects from the past can offer us much to learn today.

A Brief History of Borders: Lessons From Stone Walls through the DMZ

"The setting of boundaries is always a political act. Boundaries determine membership: someone must be inside and someone outside. Boundaries also create and delineate space to facilitate the activities and purposes of political, economic, and social life. Using physical space to create social place is a long and deep American tradition."[4]

~ Edward J. Blakely and Mary Gail Snyder, *Fortress America*

While their is a book about gated communities and the harm these residential developments do to civic space, the authors chose the idea of *Fortress America* for a reason larger than the analogy of gated communities and walled cities alone. The term "Fortress America" is actually a historical reference to advocates of an isolationist foreign policy in the United States in the 1930s and 1940s, prior to World War II. Charles Lindberg, the famous aviator, championed this point of view in American politics of the times, becoming a spokesman for the "America First" movement. He and his colleagues believed in a Fortress America based on the natural "walls" of the Atlantic and Pacific Oceans, keeping the country secure by requiring a warring enemy to travel across these oceans to attack us. The alternative, sending our troops to Europe, would leave our armed forces weaker and more vulnerable to attack. His "America First" speech, delivered on April 23, 1941, includes this reference to his definition of national security:

Practically every difficulty we would face in invading Europe becomes an asset to us in defending America. Our enemy, and not we, would then have the problem of transporting millions of troops across the ocean and landing them on a hostile shore. They, and not we, would have to furnish the convoys to transport guns and trucks and munitions and fuel across 3,000 miles of water. Our battleships and submarines would then be fighting close to their home bases. We would then do the bombing from the air and the torpedoing at sea. And if any part of an enemy convoy should ever pass our Navy and our air force, they would still be faced with the guns of our coast artillery and behind them the divisions of our Army.[5]

History shows that this belief in building defenses behind national borders, in order to prevent enemies from attacking a country by assuring an overwhelming response, failed as a military strategy during World War II. In fact, it had already failed in places like France with its Maginot Line, and would fail a few months later when the Japanese attacked US warships in Pearl Harbor, Hawaii. More recently, President George W. Bush signed the *Secure Fence Act of 2006*, which authorized hundreds of miles of new fencing along the border between the United States and Mexico, the creation of additional checkpoints, barriers, and lighting, and the introduction of technological monitoring systems including cameras, satellites, and drones. President Bush claimed that "This bill will help protect the American people. This bill will make our borders more secure. It is an important step toward immigration reform ."[6] The fences erected in 2006 were not the first to be built along the US—Mexican border; the US Border Patrol began this process as early as 1990 near San Diego, California.[7] Today, the Trump Administration has ordered the Department of Homeland Security to issue a request for proposals for the design of prototype sections of the border wall then-candidate Donald Trump called for in his successful campaign for president.

Good Walls, Good Neighbors: A Timeless Debate

Still, the concept of building strong defenses behind a natural or man-made wall (the Atlantic Ocean, in Lindberg's case) goes back centuries. Throughout most of its history, when public order and even survival depended on separating livestock from crops, "Good fences make good neighbours" was an axiom that simply stated common sense. Note that fences in these early days weren't meant to keep people from each other; they were meant to keep neighbors' livestock from wandering freely and eating their neighbors' crops. This proverb may have been first recorded in *Blums' Farmer's and Planter's Almanac* in 1850, but it was almost certainly centuries old even then.[8] (It would be used years later in Robert Frost's 1914 poem, "Mending Wall.")

But how is that phrase or saying still relevant today? Senators and presidents have used this phrase to justify laws authorizing the construction and fortification of borders, as cited above. Politicians including Charles Lindberg have used it to justify retreating behind natural barriers as a means of keeping the evils of war from the American people. Magazines and academics have quoted it as well, but does anyone know that the purpose behind putting up a fence in the first place was to keep cattle and livestock from destroying crops? Fences worked to accomplish this goal, to be sure, but I believe that relying on a concept so ancient in today's world is in fact a denial of the changes brought about by technological advances over the past centuries, and now decades. Livestock may still be unable to climb walls, but every man-made wall and virtually every natural barrier has been overcome by inventions such as cannons, warships, airplanes, missiles, and electronics. Relying on walls in the face of their repeated failure is nothing short of a denial of history and—more than that— human intelligence.

This is not to say that looking back through history to witness debates about the advantages and disadvantages of walls is worth our attention. In fact, even when the survival of a community was at stake from starvation should livestock eat their crops, there has always been a push back from civic leaders about the resulting danger of walls and fences separating people and cutting of communication channels necessary for commerce, collaboration, and technological advancement. For example, in a letter from Reverend Ezekiel Rogers to John Winthrop, the first governor of the Massachusetts Bay Colony, Rogers wrote; "I have thought, that a good fence helpeth to keepe peace between neighbours; but let us take a heed that we make not a high stone wall, to keepe us from meeting."[9]

Another example is English essayist and minister Vicesimus Knox, who in 1797 translated the Spanish saying, "Una pared entre doz vezinos guarda más la amistad," which means, "A wall between both, best preserves friendship."[10] In short, we can see from past conversations and debates that the fence or wall itself was never the issue; it was the separation of people from each other that was of concern. It was important for civic leaders at the time to balance security concerns with an interest in keeping communication and social relationships open and accessible regardless of the existence of a fence or wall.

New England Stone Walls

New England soil is an endless stone reservoir. Each spring when the ice thaws, we see a new supply of granite and other stones. New England farmers used these stones to create walls around their fields, but they were constantly being destroyed by harsh winters and livestock. Farmers were constantly having to rebuild their walls in order to maintain their functionality. However, when a few decades later farmers found better land elsewhere, they abandoned their old land and the walls they had built there. "Walls that once divided fields and enclosed paddocks now crisscross woods or decay in stands of maple and white pine behind housing developments, shopping malls, and vacant lots ... the New England stone wall has become an icon of a lost and better time…."[11] In a similar way, national boundaries have virtually disappeared across western Europe.[12]

> *"He only says, 'Good fences make good neighbors.'*
> *Spring is the mischief in me, and I wonder*
> *If I could put a notion in his head:*
> *'Why do they make good neighbors? Isn't it*
> *Where there are cows? But here there are no cows.*
> *Before I built a wall I'd ask to know*
> *What I was walling in or walling out,*
> *And to whom I was like to give offense."*

~ Robert Frost, "Mending Wall," 1914[13]

Writing about two neighbors walking along the stone wall separating their two properties in the springtime, Robert Frost tells the story of how one neighbor sees no need for the wall, since all it separates now are apple and pine trees. When he asks why the wall should remain, let alone be repaired, his neighbor only repeats the old adage about good walls and good neighbors. In a way, Frost's poem is about the ways reconciliation happens. The two neighbors' unresolved conversation is neither an appeal to tear down walls or to ignore them, but rather to ask questions of them. The poem asks readers to look at their own motives whenever they make or remake a boundary, to confront the tensions between power and impotence, inclusion and exclusion, separation and connection—the issues that every wall, every fence, every hedge, or every ditch embodies. "Mending Wall" is a poem is about the ethics behind a wall; it serves as a guide for today's readers even though it follows the principles of another time.

Gradually, with the advent of telegraph, the telephone, and increasingly sophisticated wireless communication media, the concept of space has moved from the physical to virtual world (even though we didn't call it by this name until late in the twentieth century). Manuel Castells defines this virtual world of social networks as the "space of flows."[14] Castells notes that each day, we see a million or more users added to "virtual" social networks spanning language, culture, and continents. What Castells calls a space of flows is no longer an abstraction, but in fact a very real space that people inhabit every day.

The growth of this virtual space of flows may seem liberating and expansive, as we often view most technological advances and the discovery of new places to explore. Yet the architect and urban planner Thomas Oles warns us to be cautious in applying these assumptions too easily. "But it is a grave error to confuse the falling of legal or technological barriers with the disappearance of boundaries. Walls have fallen for some but they have risen higher and higher for many others."[15]

In describing his space of flows, Castells says that, because of the internet and social media and networking, we no longer face restrictions of distance and time when it comes to sharing ideas and information, and that for many, the cyber world is truly the world in which they live. But it is fundamentally incorrect to confuse the removal of technological border with the fall of tangible ones. For those who do not have access to these social networks, the increasing migration of people with access to these new virtual worlds creates a new type of wall: they become even more restricted, and the borders between them and people in these virtual worlds have risen even higher.

The new walls separating people who occupy these virtual worlds from those who do not are not simply those of wealth and resources. Although the difference between the "haves" and "have nots" is a very real source of separation, so are the actions of certain governments that fear the power of freely shared ideas and the loss of control it brings. Countries like China have used new technology to restrict the flow of information into their societies because they are worried about these advancements and the rapid disappearance of social networking boundaries. They have replaced physical boundaries with cyber walls. It is also worth noting that other less economically powerful countries have also applied technology to reinforce their walls. Beginning with Eastern Europe in the 1950s and continuing today in Zambia, they have constructed electrified barbed wire fences to block people from escaping out of their countries (Eastern Europe), or from seeking refuge from their neighboring country (Zambia). The political scientist Wendy Brown sees this as a kind of last gasp of national sovereignty in an age of increasing globalization, with walls becoming more theatrical props than effective boundaries against an irresistible tide.[16]

Examples of fences, walls, and buffer zones

Whether we are truly entering a time when international boundaries are disappearing in the face of increasing globalization, it is worth looking at the ways boundaries have evolved in their own history of technological advancement. The study of these walls, their materials and construction, and the political will to build them, is a fascinating story in and of itself. For our purposes, let us say that while there have been many different types of borders throughout history, most have served the same purpose even as they have used different methodologies. For example, the fence between India and Pakistan is a simple fence separating both countries: nothing more, nothing less. As noted earlier, there are already many miles of fences running along the border between the United States and Mexico. In this case, there is a fence on the US side, and then a few feet away, there is a fence on the Mexican side, with a small zone in between. The older but more technologically developed border wall separating Communist Eastern Europe from the West—the Berlin Wall—is a notorious historical artifact that served its purpose for over three decades, but ultimately failed to stem the flow of ideas that caused the political philosophy behind the wall to crumble while the wall stood, waiting to be demolished afterwards. The Berlin Wall started off as a simple fence, and it kept growing and expanding until it became a wall, with spotlights, guard posts, barbed wire, and soldiers with machine guns. Today in Palestine and Israel there is a huge wall, but missiles, mortars, and individual terrorists still manage to cross it at will. Then there is the Great Wall of China, the ancient mother of all walls, which was used to separate civilization from barbarians for centuries. Still, the wall functioned not only as a barrier; it was also occupiable and used for trade. Another boundary in the news in 2017 is the Demilitarized Zone (DMZ) between North and South Korea. With all the rhetoric and bluster from political leaders on both sides, the DMZ is actually a buffer zone between the two countries, functioning as a place where needed dialogue and communication can occur between the leaders of both countries as a means for defusing crises. Even in this most tense and extreme case of a border wall, an international boundary presents the opportunity for people to connect, communicate, and even collaborate. If there is a natural desire for people to gather at such places, why not capitalize on that human tendency to create a space that is more welcoming for such interaction and connectivity? Why not consider border cities instead of border walls?

The Evolution of Urbanity: From Medieval Walls to Border Cities

A Medieval Walled City

Beginning in medieval times, after the fall of ancient civilizations like Greece and Rome in the West, cities originally came into being as the intersection of three urban elements: the market, the church, and the home. In economies that were largely agrarian, crops would be bought and sold in the city's marketplace, and the rise of civic society—laws, the arts, and education, for example—centered around the church. These two elements, the market and the church, were the center of early cities and needed to be protected from marauders or invading armies. Homes might be impossible to defend, given the fact that they were likely dispersed over farmlands surrounding the city, so medieval city design evolved with the construction of defensible walls around the other two urban features—the market and the church. In times of attack, residents could gather behind these walls for safety and to defend these two vital urban resources from destruction.

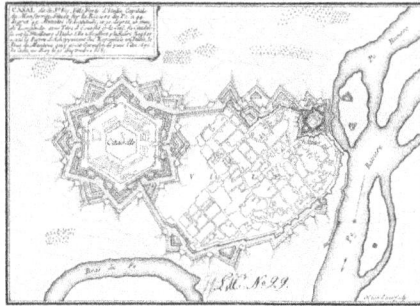

The Next Step in Urban Design: The Star-Shaped City

This sort of system worked in terms of defense until the invention of gunpowder and the guns and cannons that came with it. On a more positive note, the development of urban centers brought with it a more vibrant and diverse marketplace, creating a need for more than a simple space for buying and selling crops and livestock. Blacksmiths making tools for a sufficiently large number of farmers could set up their shops and live in the cities, as could the priests, brothers, and nuns who would teach children in the city's schools. Industries such as garment-making and woodworking might also create a growing number of urban residents who would never need to leave the city in order to earn a living. Star-shaped cities would develop the kind of hub-and-spoke structure we see even today in many American and European cities, as new residents moved into town and occupied expanding concentric circles of urban space. New walls would need to be built further from the center of town, and defenses were no longer a simple wall to keep people out; there would be a need for places to locate defense guns atop the walls, instead of a simple parapet for soldiers to occupy as lookouts in times of peace and to shoot down at invaders in times of war. The guns would require stronger foundations for support, and would also need to be able to swivel so they could fire at enemies whether they were far away or just outside the walls. Their forward positions along the city wall are what give the city its star shape.

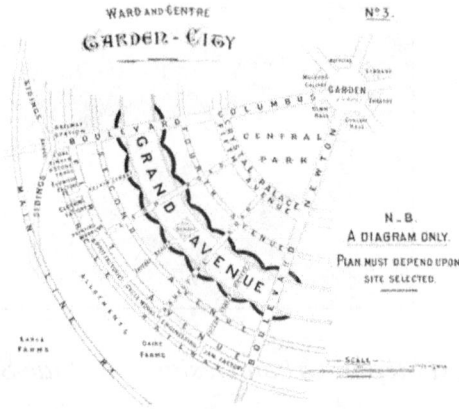

The Garden City: Open Spaces for Residents; Walls for Forts Alone

While the concept of "Garden City" can refer to a specific design movement around the turn of the twentieth century—one that sought to eliminate the difference between town and country by uniting the two in a single urban space—we are using the term to define urban spaces that have developed beyond the point in which a wall around them is practical, given the size of the city requiring an exterior wall, and also given the futility of a wall in protecting it from modern weaponry. Visitors to Rome and other European cities can see for themselves how the remnants of ancient walls may still stand, but have been pierced by roadways and buildings as the city grew beyond the limits of the wall and the wall did what they always do—it became a barrier to connections, collaboration, and communication among city residents. Tearing it down or removing sections of it became a necessary part of urban growth and design.

For a time, as exterior urban walls became obsolete, they were replaced by walled forts constructed on the outskirts of town, where armies could be garrisoned and large guns could be placed as defenses for the city even without a barrier wall around the entire town. In coastal cities, these forts would be built in the harbor, to protect against naval invasion. Forts built for military use only, and not to protect a central market or church, would also become more common along borders between countries, along transportation routes that

94

invading armies might use for attack. With this "outplacement" of defensive military bases, cities were freed from the constraints of ancient defensive walls; but at the same time, by the middle of the twentieth century, they became vulnerable to aerial attacks that no wall could prevent. Walls would become increasingly specialized, useful in restricting movement of people on foot and in vehicles, but would never again serve as effective protection against military attack.

The rise of large cities would bring with it the realization that there are other dangers residents face beyond attack by foreign "others." Crime became an increasing danger, one that could be mitigated by urban design that adds to the security of residents in new and creative ways.

Reducing Crime Through Urban Design

Oscar Newman, an American architect and urban planner, wrote his groundbreaking book, *Defensible Space*, in the 1970s. In that and subsequent works, Newman defined a design concept that involves residents as active component of a neighborhood's defense and law enforcement system. He learned from crime statistics in New York City that high-rise housing projects were more dangerous than neighborhoods where structures were only a few stories tall. From the simple conclusion that proximity to the streets is related to increased safety for residential neighborhoods, he developed a theory that includes four reasons why this is the case, and how these reasons can be incorporated into urban design. They are:

1. Territoriality: One's home is sacred.

2. Natural Surveillance: Residents' ability to see what's happening in the neighborhood.

3. Image: Physical design that instills a sense of security.

4. Milieu/Environment: Surrounding amenities that affect security (for example, proximity to a police station).

Newman assumed that since people are naturally motivated to protect their own territory, that instinct can be incorporated into good urban design. Clearly defining spaces in terms of which are private (and to whom they belong), which were public and available to anyone, and which were in a "middle ground" in which they could be used with the owner's permission, helps establish a clear definition of which territory a resident can be expected to own and protect.

In order to help residents defend the spaces for which they feel ownership, they need to be able to relate to it on a personal level. The opposite of this feeling is why Newman believed crime rates were higher in high rises, where residents live too far above the streets to believe it is their responsibility to take care of them. On a more practical level, natural surveillance can be applied in the design of urban spaces by creating housing where living room windows face front yards, or where parking lots are well lit. People who can see the nonprivate parts of their neighborhoods are more likely to defend them.

Making any residential neighborhood, including low-income projects, welcoming and pleasing to the eye is also an important element of Newman's design theory. Purely utilitarian designs that concentrate many residents on a small plot of land and do so without communicating a sense that the space has value beyond warehousing poor people is an invitation to neglect by not only the community at large, but by the residents who live there. Without a sense of ownership, they cannot be expected to participate in the monitoring and protection of their residential space.

The same can be said for the milieu in which a residential development is located. Not everyone can live next to a police station, but design that takes into consideration the harmony between housing and its surroundings is an important element in creating spaces that encourage residents to feel responsible for defending. Thinking about a residential development's milieu includes not only physical considerations such as the height of a building or the location of windows and lighting, it also includes creation of opportunities for social milieus. Gathering spaces for residents can instill a sense of shared responsibility and a kind of "home base" from which residents can observe and potentially challenge intruders. Employees, such as parking lot attendants, doormen, shopkeepers in retail spaces, or even bus drivers, can also expand the number of people who feel ownership for a residential space and participate in its monitoring and defense.[17]

On Walls and Cities: If Connectivity Always Prevails, Why Not Design for It?

"There are many boundaries in the world that separate what should be inseparable, divide what should be indivisible. Walls and fences break apart families, communities, and livelihoods, and make daily existence inconvenient, humiliating, or intolerable for millions. They project the power of the strong over the weak, the rich over the poor."[18]

~ Thomas Oles, *Walls: Enclosures and Ethics in the Modern Landscape*

As many have learned throughout history, separation does not create security. Physical barriers crumble, become obsolete, or simply fail when tested. As Reverend Ezekiel Rogers told John Winthrop in Colonial Massachusetts, we must take care that a wall is never so high that it keeps us from meeting. The Great Wall of China, while it always included spaces for commerce and communication from its earliest days, no longer separates any of us from each other; now it is a tourist attraction that brings people together. And as we have learned from Oscar Newman and his concept of defensible spaces, providing the opportunity for people to take part in the occupation and defense of a space is a good idea. Just as the best way to maintain a building is to occupy it, the best way to defend a border is to occupy it as well. It is time to consider the idea that border cities are a better and more sustainable way to accomplish the stated reasons for constructing a border wall.

The issues of how to reconcile the incentives for employers and workers to join in the challenge of building and occupying a border city, or to rationalize the differences between systems of health care, education, and the legal systems in the United States and Mexico, are formidable and will take time to solve. But to use these objections as a reason to dismiss the idea that cities are better than walls is to condemn ourselves to build another temporary solution to a permanent problem: how do we incorporate the natural desire for people to connect with each other, to collaborate with each other, and to communicate with each other, into the design for a border that is truly secure?

The forces that have led to this evolution have gotten ahead of the way we organize our cities, and—by extension—the borders between our own cities and nations and those occupied by other people. Transportation has become more rapid and everyone is mobile; people are not dangerous in ways that cannot be defended through connectivity instead of separation, and ideas can be transmitted without human movement at all. Walls are obsolete. It is time for border cities. In an attempt to frame the issues that must be addressed in their early formation, following are six design concepts from Maki Fumihiko and Rocco Yim in *Reconnecting Cultures: The Architecture of Rocco Design.*

Imagining a Solution: Design Considerations for Border Cities

"There is no place in a city that can't be better. There is no toad that can't be a princess, no frog that can't become a prince."[19]

~ Jaime Lerner

To begin our challenge of transforming the toad of a static border wall into a beautiful princess of a vibrant border city, let's explore the following six architectural concepts included in Rocco design.

1. Identity

The real identity of a building can only be born of a successful resolution of its content and its use. The beginning of any design—whether it is a building, a commercial development, or an entire city—can be inspired by traditional spatial strategies and the formal configuration of spaces, both man-made and natural. As design continues, it should move toward an outcome that takes these formal configurations and allows them to evolve in order to fit contemporary and anticipated uses and needs.[20] This is why there can be no single prototype for any border city; each will be a customized solution based on the content of its urban spaces, the formal requirements for specific types of architectural spaces, and the unique use and needs of that particular city and its equally singular environment, both natural and societal. Each city will have its own fingerprint.

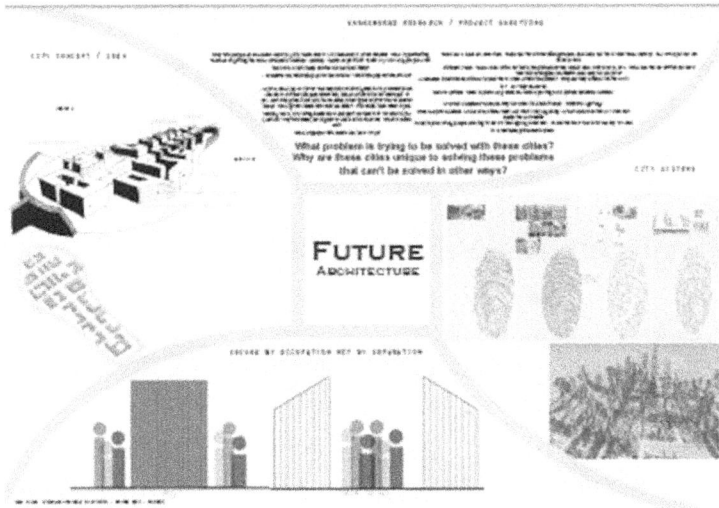

Every Border City will Connect People with Each Other in it own Individual Way

To reinforce the unique nature of each border city, we have used the symbolic analogy of a fingerprint to define its strategic design. Every human being's fingerprint establishes our unique identity, despite the overall similarity in the shape and the multibillion number of ongoing growth of human being extracting the shape of a human finger. In the same way, the identity of each border city will carry deep meaning as its own developed space that can host several architectural envelopes reflecting the sustainability and exploring the connectivity of its residents and the way their city connects them with each other and the world.

2. Spatiality

Our perception of space is shaped by our history. It is reflective of how people lived, used and appreciated spaces in the past, and how this informs our ideas for how new spaces will be occupied and function over time. Spatial arrangements such as those between buildings and open spaces on a citywide scale, or between the indoor and outdoor spaces of an individual development, provide new opportunities for very different building typologies. This can be clearly observed in buildings such as hotels, museums, and libraries; these formal design concepts will also serve as starting points for the physical design of a new border city and its neighborhoods, commercial zones, and civic spaces.[21]

3. Community

Schools and culture districts are important ways in which life is breathed into the buildings and infrastructure of an urban environment. They capture the spirit of togetherness and express it through an architectural proposition. Considerations of how to design for community needs and uses bring about more than a sense of belonging and security. They create enhanced opportunities for social exchange and communication. Alternatively, all a wall can do is create barriers in the way of social exchange and communication. While people have been known to create these spaces on their own despite a wall or even urban design that is ignorant of community considerations, we have seen that thinkers like Newman and Oles can inform design that welcomes and enhances the vibrancy and connectivity that a healthy city can provide.[22]

4. Density

From time to time, the condition of density has been tempered by concerns for environmental and spatial improvement as open spaces, light, and air have become increasingly positive urban attributes. In the past, this has been due to public health concerns; today it includes values such as aesthetics and sustainability. Instead of conflicting with these values, an optimum condition of density could be used to foster vibrancy and energy. Density can serve to enhance access and convenience, creating an urban vitality with the optimum concentration of events and happenings to increase opportunities for connectivity and communication.[23]

5. Connectivity

Cities encompass a set of conditions under which people, objects, and information collide and interact. The extent to which such collision becomes productive is a measure of how successfully the city works as an urban space. Connectivity is not just physical linkage: it also needs to be visual and spiritual. More importantly, the fusion of architecture with the public use of space requires creativity in design that will enhance the dynamics of movement, physical encounters, and interaction.[24]

6. Materiality

Understanding of the properties of materials and the appropriateness of their selection must be consistent with a building's purpose—defined not just in terms of constructability or appropriateness, but also in terms of their ability to enhance space and form, and their power to evoke emotions and sensual responses. In an age where the world is increasingly connected and homogenous, creating a unique regional presence in architectural design hinges on a relevant balancing of values: those between the past and the present, and those that are local and universal. Herein lies the essence of sustainability and authenticity in architecture, and the reason behind the following proposal to the Department of Homeland Security to build a border city instead of a wall.[25]

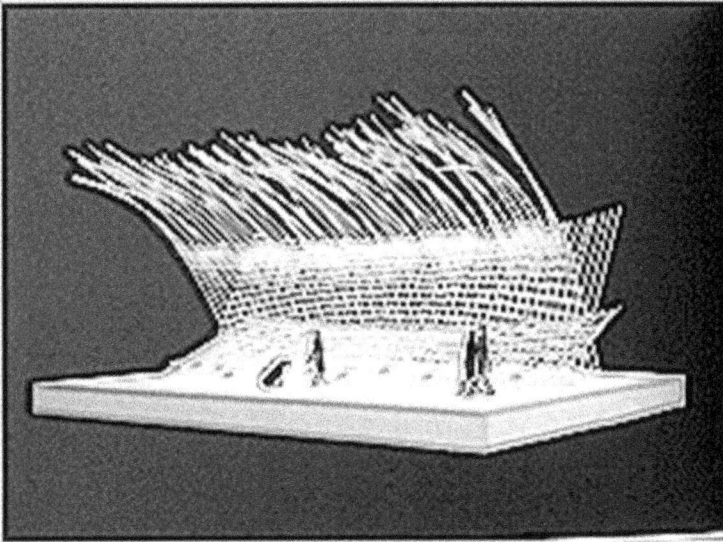

A Proposal to the US Department of Homeland Security

As final step in our case for building border cities instead of a wall between the United States and Mexico is a proposal submitted to the Department of Homeland Security (DHS) in early 2017. The proposal provides a solution for border protection that, in keeping with DHS's specific requirements, includes a static wall. But it also reinforces and empowers the wall by augmenting it with communities whose residents will protect the wall, their city, and the surrounding lands, in keeping with the design concepts and philosophies introduced in previous pages. To state it once again, just as the best way to maintain a building is to occupy it, the best way to secure a border is also to occupy it.

These border cities, with their critical issues addressed and agreed to by both countries, can carry the positive attributes of both sides of the border. For example, a free trade zone, or freedom of movement of people without formal border crossings into and out of the cities and each country without crossing to the other country, can provide protection that is superior to any cost-benefit calculations for the static wall regardless of its cost. Over time, border protection and security will be governed by residents of the cities who will, as Oscar Newman points out, have ownership and interest in maintaining the safety of places where they know they belong.

The concept of border cities has the potential to be demonstrably successful. And because it is an American idea and much of the world still turns to the United States for innovation and creative solutions, the concept of a border city can be exported for use in other countries in the same way previous American ideas have been adopted and shared worldwide.

In an ideal world, there would be a government agency that would be able to review proposals like those requested by the Department of Homeland Security to determine their value in terms of whether they are political or corrupt in nature. While we see this potential government organization as one that would contribute far more value than whatever the current administration believes a border wall will contribute to the United States, we are realistic enough to understand that the new agency we propose should not be established in the place of any other government agency. We believe that, as the United States of America considers a project that is primarily political in nature, taking the first steps toward the status quo in other countries where project managers have no chance of appealing to a higher authority, there is another answer. It involves the creation of a government agency where project managers like Roberto Rodriguez in Santa Cruz de la Sierra, Bolivia; or Samuel Anderson in Colón, Panama, could go for help in resisting the interference from corrupt or political agendas in their projects. It also involves the establishment of procedures for licensing and accrediting project managers to ensure that the profession is composed of, well ... professionals.

Writing a proposal that replaces the Department of Homeland Security's request for the design of a wall with a solution that we believe is better—*border cities*—is one of many acts an individual designer or project manager can take to resist a political agenda in the world as we know it today. After reading our proposal, please consider the ideas we put forth in the final chapter for the establishment of an organization that can take on powerful political or corrupt forces in a way no individual project manager can. The time for this government organization is now, and the place for it is in the United States.

Yasser Osman & Yara Osman

Proposal for Construction of a US-Mexico Border City
Instead of a Wall

Build a Border that Brings People Together

An Alternative to the Mexican-US Border Wall

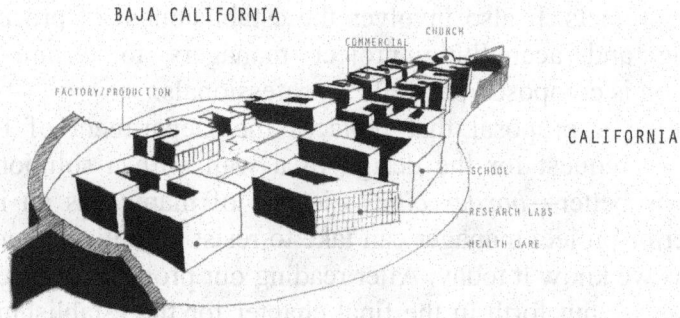

Linear border cities will provide services and opportunities to citizens of both countries.

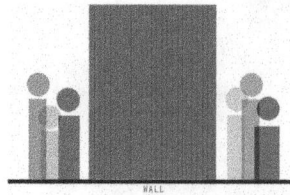

Simple walls separate people from each other.

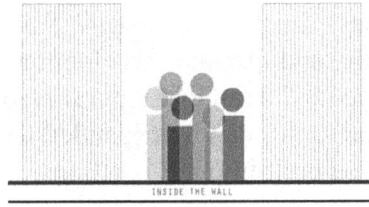

INSIDE THE WALL

Border cities foster international collaboration.

US Customs and Border Protection
Department of Homeland Security
Washington, DC

Dear People,

We are happy to submit our conceptual design for the construction contract you are seeking to award along the US-Mexican border. Please note that while our proposal includes several miles of the wall you specify, our primary idea is for a linear border city, with buildings such as schools, health clinics, research centers, and high-tech manufacturing facilities. Our idea would change the concept of the future US-Mexican border from one of confrontation and tension along a static and unproductive wall to a vibrant center of collaboration and coexistence along an innovative linear urban center.

At several locations along the border, these cities will be built within a narrow space that is neither Mexico nor the United States, but is open to citizens from both countries who seek education, health care, employment, or a place to innovate and create new technologies. They can come and go as they please from their homes to these new linear cities, since they would never need to cross an international border in order to benefit from the human services and employment opportunities available within them.

Buildings would be built to current US and Mexican standards for schools, health care facilities, research centers, and other facilities; the two countries would collaborate on the number, size, location, and

109

nature of these cities. Each city would feature its own unique constellation of public and private development in response to the needs of local residents and available natural resources. If the concept proves to be successful, cities can be expanded to nearby open land, or new border cities can be built in other locations.

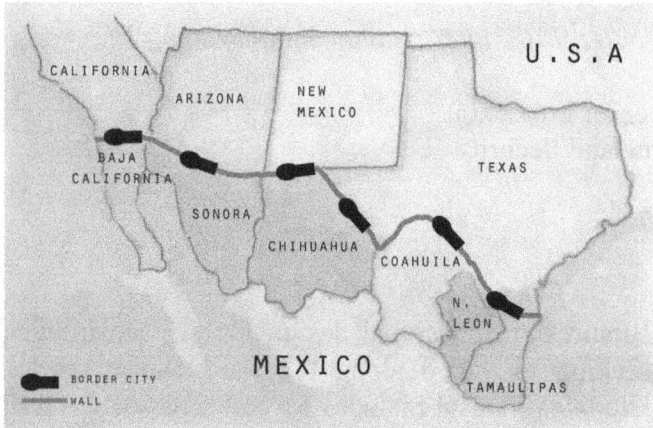

The US-Mexican Border with proposed border cities.

We believe our ideas add value that will enhance the long-term success of your project:

1. **Marketing**: If Mexico is going to pay for the project, they should realize some benefit from their investment. Paying for education, health care, jobs, and new technology will be a much easier sell than a static wall.

2. **Return on Investment**: A static wall will at best generate no income during its useful life. At worst, it will need an annual maintenance budget for normal wear and tear. A border city with a good balance of private-sector businesses and public-sector services can produce goods and services for citizens of both countries, and build a workforce for tomorrow through its schools

and technology centers. Investment in factories and technology laboratories could be encouraged by private corporations instead of requiring government funding.

3. **Jobs**: The development of private-sector businesses and public-sector services will create jobs for citizens of both countries in numbers that will far outpace the number of people to be employed in patrolling a border wall.

4. **Immigration control**: By locating schools, health clinics, and jobs in a neutral space that is neither the United States nor Mexico, border cities will reduce the need for people seeking employment, education, or health care to leave either country for these opportunities. Instead, they will commute back and forth from their homes to the border city.

5. **Land use**: Walls and their adjacent security zones require a linear "no man's land" to enforce border control and prevent illegal crossings. Border cities will transform these barren spaces into productive communities.

6. **Future sustainability**: Borders change. Seventy years ago, the border between Germany and France was the site of fortifications, gun emplacements, and ultimately, war and carnage. Thirty years ago, there was a wall between East and West Germany. Neither of these locations requires a wall today. Our proposal would eliminate the costly construction of a wall that is likely going to be obsolete in a few decades, requiring it to be dismantled (at additional cost). Each border city can expand along the border, or even into each country if, as we anticipate, the opportunities they create attract more of their citizens.

7. **Replication**: The United States and Mexico are not the only countries with a border that can use a new idea. By creating a new concept of an international frontier that is not a barrier but a center for cooperation, innovation, and opportunity, the Department of Homeland Security can create a model to inspire other countries to follow our lead in changing the nature of their boundaries that will reduce international tensions and replace conflict with collaboration.

We note that your request for proposals calls for the development of prototype sections of a wall that would be built along the entire border of our two countries by the successful bidder. Our proposal is scalable in nature; our prototype concept includes the initial development of two border cities in separate locations. Each of them would be supported by public-private partnerships including the Mexican and US federal governments, the states on either side of the border (Texas and Coahuila, for example; or Arizona and Sonora), and international corporations seeking to invest in these new cities.

Based on the success of these first two prototypes, additional cities can be sited along the border to replace sections of its wall with vibrant, lively new communities. Over time, when our border cities concept is up and running, we believe it will demonstrably outperform both the status quo and any future construction involving a wall.

Respectfully submitted,

Yasser and Yara Osman
Pottstown, Pennsylvania

Chapter 6

A Call for the Federal Department of Project Investigation (FPI)

"The whole difference between construction and creation is exactly this: that a thing constructed can only be loved after it is constructed; but a thing created is loved before it exists."
~ Charles Dickens

In the first five chapters of this book, we have traveled with project managers from Santa Cruz de la Sierra, Bolivia, in the present day to Colón, Panama, in 1907, visiting with them as they struggled to manage major international construction and development projects in the face of corrupt or political interference. Then we have journeyed back to the present day along the border between the United States and Mexico, to explore the ways in which a political agenda can interfere with the value a major international project can bring to society. We have also taken an academic look at how project management standards can be applied to help managers learn the true nature of the projects they are managing, and how this knowledge can be used to identify the boundaries beyond which they can never manage, while allowing managers to focus on the things they can direct in order to succeed in the scope of work for which they have been hired. We have witnessed fictional stories that are based on the authors' real-life experiences, and seen the risks and dangers individual project managers face almost universally, without recourse to a higher authority to protect them or their projects from the kind of interference we have illustrated in some detail.

In this concluding chapter, it is time for us to talk about the realities of how political or corrupt interference affect projects and project managers in a way that goes beyond the experience of a single individual manager, as we have done throughout this book so far. In our opinion, while individual project managers can use the information and ideas we have introduced in this book to make choices about how

113

to proceed in a project where they find a secret scope of work and secret stakeholders managing the delivery of this secret "twin," these answers are not enough.

An individual project manager can use the information in this book to identify a corrupt or political project. But individual managers are still left with one of two choices: resign and leave the project in order to maintain their ethical standards, or stay and live with the corrupt or political agenda as best as they can, either joining in the corruption or managing around it to the best of their abilities. While each can be defended from the perspective of the individual manager, this choice should not be tolerated by a society that expects people to enter a profession that has ethical standards. And it is the responsibility of that society—not the individual project manager—to establish and defend these standards for the profession of project management. It is a choice that can no longer be made in many countries: they have already passed the point of no return, their governments either tolerating or sponsoring corrupt and political agendas in their construction and development projects. But at least today, in 2017, there are still countries where it is not too late, although it might not be too late for very long. One such place is the United States of America. We end our book with two brief stories about the choice a society can make about dealing with political or corrupt projects, and the consequences of these choices.

Qatar and the United States: Which Way Will We Go?

In early June 2017, many Americans awoke to the news that, shortly after the US president's return from a state visit to Saudi Arabia and a meeting with the Gulf Cooperation Council (GCC) Nations, several GCC members broke diplomatic ties with Qatar, citing that small country's continuing financial support for terrorism as the reason for this break. Readers of this book will be able to imagine the events that have led to this dramatic international incident: a series of corrupt and political projects that have been used to disguise support for international terrorism and programs sponsored by government "friends" of Qatar that are controversial enough to be kept secret.

The people most likely to be involved in these activities would start with the government officials and private individuals initiating the multiple examples of Qatar's secret financial support. But not far behind would be the managers in charge of the projects being used by these government officials or individuals to funnel money from Qatar to these secret destinations. They would possibly be confused or concerned by one or more of the many signs that their projects are in fact being used by secret stakeholders to fund a secret scope of work. And if they were able to determine that in fact their projects are political or corrupt in nature, they would need to make one of the two choices available to them in Qatar: resign or live with the reality of managing a corrupt or political project. There is no other option in Qatar: a project manager cannot appeal to a higher government authority for help in dealing with the consequences of a secret agenda because, as we have recently seen, several of Qatar's neighbors believe the government itself is involved in these political and corrupt agendas.

Substitute "Doha" for "Santa Cruz de la Sierra," or "Al Udeid Air Base" for "Panama Canal," change the names of any of the individuals and organizations in our fictional stories for others located in Qatar, multiply these by a factor of ten, fifty, or more, and you'll get a critical mass of secret political and corrupt projects with similar changes in scope or budget or schedule based on the interests of the people trying to funnel money through these projects for some other secret purpose. Allow this to continue for years and eventually you get to a point when the nation itself is sanctioned by its neighbors for allowing these sorts of transactions to continue. Project managers who have done business in Qatar may take some satisfaction in seeing this—a kind of "I told you so" after the fact—but in some cases, these same individuals suffered financial harm or damage to their careers for no other reason than they were caught in the middle of a corrupt project. Qatar did nothing to prevent this damage, and ultimately the powerful people behind that country's political or corrupt projects will have enough money to save themselves from personal risk. The people who have suffered are those harmed by the activities these secret projects have funded—people injured or killed by weapons bought with money from a corrupt Qatari project—and also the project managers fired for "incompetence" or imprisoned for more serious charges rooted in the corrupt political projects where they found themselves, mostly through no choice of their own. Should the sanctions against Qatar result in more serious economic damage to that country, its citizens will be the next to suffer.

*   *   *   *   *   *

Today in the United States, project managers are entering the profession with the same opportunities and risks their colleagues have faced for generations. Their careers will consist of a series of assignments, each of which will have its own chances for success or failure, and the managers' performance over a series of these assignments will be the basis for their continued employment in additional projects—larger and more challenging ones if they have done "good jobs," or smaller and less attractive assignments if they have not.

Unlike other professions like doctors, lawyers, nurses, and so on, there are no licensing or accreditation procedures for project managers. They are likely college graduates and may also have graduate school degrees, but there is no professional association or government organization in place to give them the credentials equivalent to a law degree, or a degree in medicine, or an architectural license. Project managers simply "are." We have no governing body or union that can protect our interests as members, and we have no professional licensing or accreditation to distinguish ourselves from people who simply claim they are "project managers." The time has come to change this.

Our recommendation is that the federal government step in to fill this void. We propose the creation of a Federal Project Managers Agency, one that includes a Federal Department of Project Investigation—the FPI. This agency can both establish and confer professional standards for the profession, and would also protect managers who find themselves in difficulties too large for any individual to address. Setting accreditation standards would be an important first step in recognizing the professionalism of project managers, and could be done with the help of any number of schools of management and design. These schools could work together to establish minimum standards for education, which could include courses leading to the accreditation test with far more extensive review of the concepts included in this book—both academic project management standards and techniques, and case studies to illustrate how these can be practiced in real projects. This education could also include opportunities for prospective managers to demonstrate their skills and expertise via testing and supervised service, much like those requiring doctors to serve an internship before receiving their MD.

But a potentially even more important value of this government agency, in our opinion, would be the creation of the FPI, which would be available for project managers to engage in reviewing any project in which they are working for possible political or corrupt interference, among other irregularities that might warrant government action to prevent this interference and protect managers from harm to their careers. While the specific ways in which such an agency might investigate a project to determine if it is in fact political or corrupt in nature would be exhaustive, they could begin with the ten project performance standards introduced in chapter 2 of this book.

Beyond that, however, is a more general concept we believe is useful in a broader way. This requires a brief return to our concepts of fixed and moving wealth, as introduced in *Buildings, Projects, and Babies*, and revisited briefly at the beginning of this book. Again, fixed wealth is composed of the things a project both uses and produces in the activity of a construction or development project. Fixed wealth begins with wooden beams, concrete, prefabricated steel frame walls, HVAC systems, etc. It concludes with a functioning luxury shopping mall, mixed-use hotel, residential, and office tower, or an airport or a major highway. Moving wealth is composed of the human beings and the knowledge, skills, and talents they bring with them throughout their careers. Man creates fixed wealth, while only God can create moving wealth.

The FPI would best succeed by concentrating its efforts on investigating fixed wealth, not moving wealth. This may seem counterintuitive to readers at first glance. Criminal intent, and the analogous corrupt or political agendas that interfere with large international construction and development projects, are typically found by looking within human behavior and intent—in short, they are elements of moving wealth, even if the term "wealth" is itself corrupted in these cases. But investigating flaws in moving wealth is better left to criminal lawyers, psychologists, and even philosophers. Starting the investigation of a potentially corrupt or political project with a look into moving wealth is the wrong approach; it is far more difficult to prove intent, and far easier for a corrupt or political individual to hide a secret agenda behind a convincing defense of their intended moving wealth. That is, after all, why corrupt and political projects are so prevalent in the world today.

But if the FPI were to begin by looking at the project's fixed wealth, just as we have argued in this book, there will be inexplicable irregularities that require further questions, and an open investigation of these questions will in most cases lead to the discovery of the true nature of a project. Using our delivery room analogy one last time, we say, "Look at the baby. It may not yet be able to speak, but it will tell you a lot." Or, to use another historical analogy from *All the President's Men*, the 1976 movie based on the Watergate Scandal, "Follow the money." One of the movie's lead characters, Deep Throat, tells the investigative reporters that, by doing this—by following the money—they will discover the full extent of the crime and cover-up at the heart of the scandal they are investigating. We agree, although in the case of a large international construction or development project, the trail of the money is not always the easiest place to start. After all, hiding the way in which the money is flowing is at the heart of a corrupt or political project. In these cases, it is easier to look for an irregularity in one of the ten project measurement standards from Chapter 2, and to continue from there. Eventually, a relentless look at these irregularities will *lead* investigators *to* the money.

*   *   *   *   *   *

Calling for the creating of the FPI might be a good way to end this book. But we believe there is a better way. We want to engage readers in a continuing dialogue about your experiences in projects that are, or might have, a corrupt or secret political agenda. To do this, we've created a FACEBOOK PAGE {https://www.facebook.com/GoMangers/} as a forum for these discussions, and as a way for project managers to add their voices to a support the creation of the FPI and to advocate for more support for project managers, both in the United States and throughout the world. We believe that management is a challenge on its own that can make or break any in which a manager is involved, no matter what opportunities or challenges exist. We hope that this book will open discussions about real situations that we all face as project managers, not just abstract academic talk about the *ideal* situations that all management processes are designed to support.

Specifically, we want to start our conversations on the site/page we have launched with these three important elements:

1. A list of actual or possible projects that are corrupt or secretly political.

As noted earlier in this book, the authors have experience worldwide in managing international megaprojects, including several in Qatar. At the time of this book's printing, Qatar's role in providing financial support for a number of secret political purposes has caused a break in relations with many of its neighbors and a resulting internal economic crisis that threatens its future as an international business hub in the Middle East. To get our new website/page started, we are happy to list some of the organizations with which we have worked—not to accuse any of them of anything improper or corrupt, far from it. We hope to enlist them and other companies that may have found themselves in the midst of an agenda beyond their control to participate in our movement toward more recognition, certification, and protection of the professionals in our field, and to engage in a continuing dialogue about how to lower the risks associated with corrupt or secret political projects in the future. To that end, we have created a website and invite readers to visit and post their experiences to keep our conversation relevant and up-to-date in a rapidly changing world:

FPI - Federal Project Investigation

As we were assembling a list of the projects we would contribute to the site, the coauthors engaged in a vigorous debate. One felt strongly that the names of companies, government agencies, and individuals needed to be shown, not only on the site but also in this book. The other objected strongly to doing this, believing that our book should remain focused on the reader and not ourselves. In that coauthor's view, introducing any possible listings for the Facebook page {https://www.facebook.com/GoMangers/} might preempt readers' freedom to choose their contributions by creating implied guidelines for these contributions. After much discussion and several revisions, we decided, of course, on a middle ground, which is to summarize how the country of Qatar described the rapidly growing construction sector of its economy a few years ago.

We chose a 2012 report by the commercial bank of Qatar; it provides details on current construction projects and projected investment in them. Below is a chart from that report, along with our summary of the information it provides:

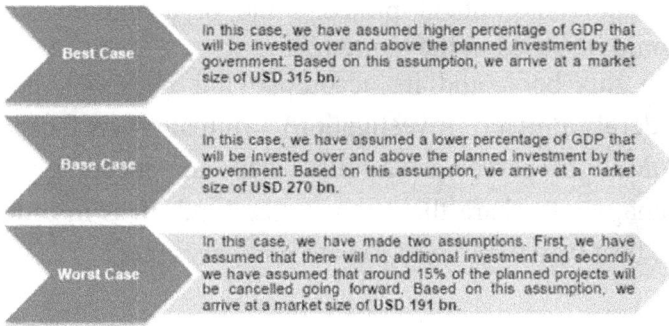

Best Case — In this case, we have assumed higher percentage of GDP that will be invested over and above the planned investment by the government. Based on this assumption, we arrive at a market size of USD 315 bn.

Base Case — In this case, we have assumed a lower percentage of GDP that will be invested over and above the planned investment by the government. Based on this assumption, we arrive at a market size of USD 270 bn.

Worst Case — In this case, we have made two assumptions. First, we have assumed that there will no additional investment and secondly we have assumed that around 15% of the planned projects will be cancelled going forward. Based on this assumption, we arrive at a market size of USD 191 bn.

Exhibit 5: Spending Patterns based on different scenarios – Forecast (USD bn)

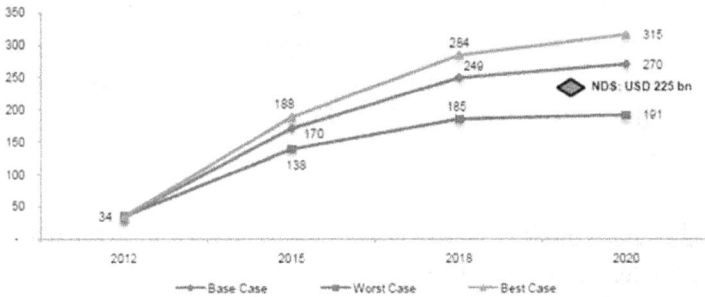

In the eight years following the report's baseline year of 2012, it forecast expenditures on projects totaling $270 billion dollars (US). Accordingly, we believe readers might want to ask:

-   How much of this money might be diverted toward a hidden political or corrupt agenda?
-   In cases where these hidden agendas were actually being funded, who would be able to report any wrongdoing other than the project manager who is responsible for monitoring the entire picture?
-   Until there is an organization that can effectively monitor projects for corrupt and/or political secret agendas, what is the best way to invite these project managers to share their experiences? (Note that we are discussing the country of Qatar, which has a track record of tolerating and possibly sponsoring

corrupt and political projects; the organization we propose would be based in the United States).
- Can this book and its accompanying Facebook page(FPI—Federal Project Investigation) {https://www.facebook.com/GoMangers/serve as a first step in encouraging project managers to share their experiences and ideas in order to find the best way to proceed toward a better future?

Instead of listing specific projects as was agreed, the coauthors believe it is worth mentioning four ways in which different organizational structures might be early indicators of possible secret agendas. We hope this simple list will help organize our introduction to the online dialogue we wish to promote, and to spark the curiosity and imagination of readers we invite to contribute to our site:

a. **Projects and international construction companies:**
The participation of large international construction companies is a norm for the megaprojects that are becoming increasingly common in today's world economy. Megaprojects are often located in countries where economies are booming, and they are also associated with mega budgets. This combination in and of itself is not an indication of the possibility of a corrupt or political secret agenda. However, when a the project is located in a country that has few or no official checks and balances to protect against financial irregularities, this third element of a megaproject makes conditions more favorable for the existence of a secret agenda.

b. **Local companies with international owners:**
In our experience, there were a number of cases in which corporations based in Qatar were owned by individuals from other countries. Again, this ownership pattern alone doesn't prove the existence of a corrupt or political agenda, but in some cases, these owners would appear rather suddenly in Qatar and would quickly be granted citizenship—a requirement for the kind of ownership

they assumed in these local corporations. When these events were followed in short order by the award of megaprojects to the corporations owned by these new Qatari citizens, we were at first confused. This confusion multiplied when the companies owned by these new individuals became more difficult to reach and their decisions were announced in ways that were no longer consistent with prior agreements.

c. Domestic companies owned by native citizens

Another pattern we have observed involves companies that are wholly owned by the country's citizens and have been for many years, or even for generations. These companies may suddenly expand in size within their field of expertise, such as a small engineering or construction firm becoming part of a team managing a new megaproject. Alternatively, they may be awarded a contract for work that is entirely unrelated to their previous business model—for example, a clothing retailer suddenly becoming a provider of HVAC systems, or winning a contract to transport building materials and construction workers to the site of a megaproject. Similar to the examples cited above, when the surprising growth of a domestic corporation is followed by difficulties in maintaining the communication channels necessary for effective project management, this may be a sign that there is a secret agenda in addition to a project's official purpose.

d. A government organization

There are also projects that are initiated and managed by government agencies exempt from standard bidding procedures. Sometimes these are unavoidable consequences associated with projects that involve state secrets, such as military bases or facilities requiring significant security features, such as legislative headquarters or the official residences of government officials. However, even in these cases, the agencies responsible for the project are typically listed in some way, and they have websites, press liaisons, or other public representation. Most official government projects are also run by organizations that operate under clear lines of authority that are traceable to the president, prime minister, legislature, or other head of state. When there is no way to find a government agency or the officials who control it in any of these public-facing communication channels, there is a significant possibility that the agency and people involved are part of a secret corrupt or political project operating behind the scenes.

2. A call for the formal creation of the FPI

We would like to engage the current president of the United States in our cause. He as much as anyone has experience in the organization and management of international construction and development projects, and therefore understands the risks posed by corrupt and secret political agendas. He is also as likely as anyone to recognize the presence of a secret corrupt or political agenda, since he has worked in a number of countries where these agendas are more common than they are in the United States and other more democratic nations. We believe that given his experience and his interest in creating American leadership for best practices in big business throughout the world, he can be a key ally in establishing the FPI, and can contribute toward its design and successful operations based on his long career in international construction and development.

3. Creation of an Online Educational Game about Project Management

We invite readers and visitors to our website to contribute toward the development of an online game that can be a new way of educating professionals in our field—particularly individuals who have experience in these ventures and might partner with us in creating these new educational tools. Consistent with our general introduction of the ways a project's organizational structure might indicate the presence of a secret agenda, we offer this general overview of the way one of these games might be structured: it could invite players to choose between two projects. Neither of them will be identified during the selection process, but one will involve a secret corrupt or political agenda, while the other will not. At each level of the game, the player's job is to conduct normal project management activities such as reviewing the progress of a building under construction and identify defects, or to set up and monitor standard communication channels among team members. Depending on the specific examples included in each game—and whether each player is managing a corrupt project or a "normal" one—the results of these activities will lead to continued success or increasing difficulties. Some of these difficulties will be associated with possible corruption, while others will be the kinds of issues that arise in even the best of projects, such as delays caused by bad weather, a labor strike, or materials shortages. The goal for each player will be to complete the project within schedule, budget, and quality standards, and to make a profit. Over time, the player managing the corrupt project will face the choice of complying with an implicitly corrupt agenda, or in deciding to declare the project to be corrupt. Scoring could be structured so it is possible for the manager of the corrupt project to "win" by either declaring the project to be corrupt, or to say nothing and pocket a share of the project's secret, corrupt transfers of money. At the conclusion of the game, players can discuss the choices they have made and the consequences of these decisions as a way of increasing their knowledge about project management strategies and techniques, and how these elements of their profession perform (or fail to perform) in the face of secret political or corrupt agendas.

*   *   *   *   *   *

"Follow the money." It worked as a way to reveal the corruption behind the Watergate scandal over forty years ago. Today we say, "Follow the project." It will lead to the discovery of the true nature of a political or corrupt project. And, before it is too late, a national government committed to preventing the spread of such projects within its own borders can use this knowledge to keep its projects, and ultimately its economic and political system, free.

Thank you for reading our book and good luck to all project managers.

References

[1] "Construction of the first transcontinental railroad," *Panama Canal Railway Company website*, http://www.panarail.com/en/history/index.html, accessed June 8, 2017.

[2] Cook, Peter, *Reconnecting Cultures: The Architecture of Rocco Design*. 2014, London, Artifice Books on Architecture, p. 7.

[3] *Ibid.*, pp. 6, 7.

[4] Blakely, E.J., and Snyder, M.G., *Fortress America*. 2010, Washington, DC, The Brookings Institution Press, p. 1.

[5] Lindberg, Charles, *America First Speech*, April 23, 1941.

[6] White House. *Fact Sheet: The Secure Fence Act Of 2006. 2006*. Web. April 29, 2017.

[7] Monteagudo, Merrie. "Chronology: San Diego-Tijuana Border Region." *San Diego Union-Tribune*. Web April 29, 2017.

[8] Baker, A., "Good Fences Make Good Neighbors" *Journal of American Folklore* 64, no.254 (1951) p. 421.

[9] Apperson, G. L. *The Wordsworth Dictionary Of Proverbs*. 1st ed. 2006, Ware, UK: Wordsworth Reference. p. 241.

[10] Knox, Vicesimus, *Elegant Extracts, or Useful and Entertaining Passages in Prose, Selected for the Improvement of Young Persons*, 1797; reproduced London: J. Johnson, 1808. p. 186.

[11] Oles, T., *Walls: Enclosures and Ethics in the Modern Landscape*, 1st ed. 2015. Chicago: The University of Chicago Press. p. 5.

[12] *Ibid*, p. 10.

[13] Frost, Robert. *The Poems of Robert Frost*. 1946, New York, NY, The Modern Library, p. 35.

[14] Castells, M., *The Rise of Network Society*. 1996, Malden, MA, Blackwell Publishing, pp. 376– 428.

[15] *Op Cit*, Oles, p. 10.

[16] Brown, W. *Walled States, Waning Sovereignty*. 2010, Cambridge, MA. MIT Press.

[17] Newman, Oscar. *Defensible Space*. 1977. London, Architectural Press.

[18] *Op Cit.*, Oles, p. 13.

[19] Lerner, Jaime. BrainyQuote.com, Xplore Inc, 2017. https://www.brainyquote.com/quotes/quotes/j/jaimelerne560345.html, accessed April 29, 2017.

[20] *Op Cit*, Cook, pp. 20–32.

[21] *Ibid,* pp. 62–72.

[22] *Ibid*, pp. 88–96.

[23] *Ibid*, pp. 124–134.

[24] *Ibid*, pp. 152–166.

[25] *Ibid*, pp. 196–202.

Other books by the Author.

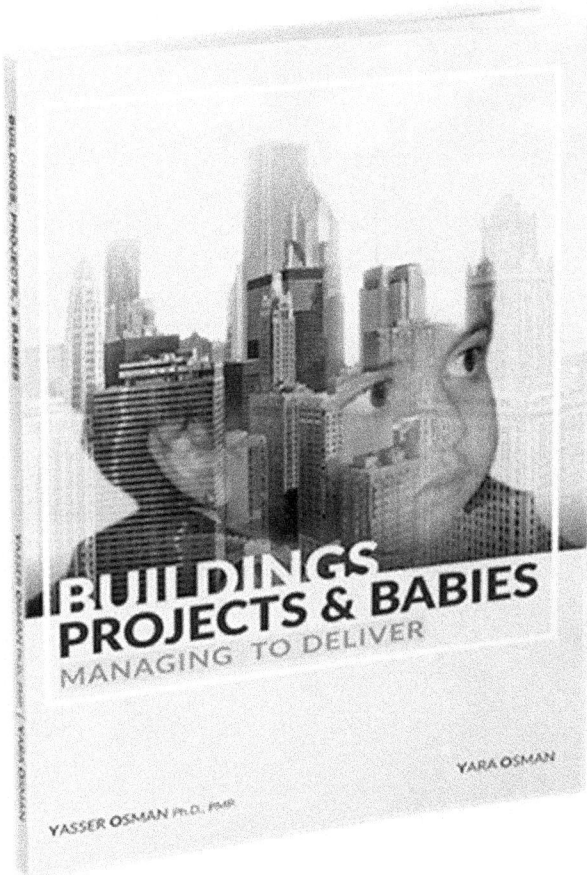

129

www.ingramcontent.com/pod-product-compliance
Lightning Source LLC
Chambersburg PA
CBHW071701210326
41597CB00017B/2272